Chilean Voices

Activists Describe their Experiences of the Popular Unity Period

VIVA NUESTRO
GobiERNO
P. R. C. POPULAR

COLIN HENFREY AND BERNARDO SORJ

CHILEAN VOICES

CHILEAN VOICES

Activists describe their Experiences
of the Popular Unity Period

RECORDED, EDITED AND TRANSLATED BY

Colin Henfrey

Lecturer in Sociology at the University of Liverpool

AND

Bernardo Sorj

THE HARVESTER PRESS

First published in 1977 by
THE HARVESTER PRESS LIMITED
Publisher: John Spiers
2 Stanford Terrace, Hassocks, Sussex.

ISBN 0 85527 869 2 (paper)
ISBN 0 85527 879 X (cloth)

Copyright © by C. Henfrey and B. Sorj, 1977

Photoset by Red Lion Setters, Holborn, London
Printed by Redwood Burn Limited, Trowbridge, Wiltshire

British Library Cataloguing in Publication Data

Henfrey, Colin
    Chilean voices.
    Bibl. — Index.
    ISBN 0-85527-869-2
    ISBN 0-85527-879-X Pbk
    1. Title 2. Sorj, Bernardo
    983'.064
    Chile — History — 1920-
    Chile — Politics and government — 1970-

Caminante, son tus huellas
el camino, y nada más;
caminante, no hay camino,
se hace camino al andar.
Al andar se hace camino,
y al volver la vista atrás
se ve la senda que nunca
se ha de volver a pisar....

As you make your way, it's your own footsteps
which make the way, and they alone;
as you make your way, there is no way,
the way is simply where you go.
Your going simply makes the way,
till looking back the way you came,
you see behind you the narrow path
which you will never take again....

— From *Campos de Castilla* (The Fields of Castille)
by Antonio Machado, (1875-1939)

Contents

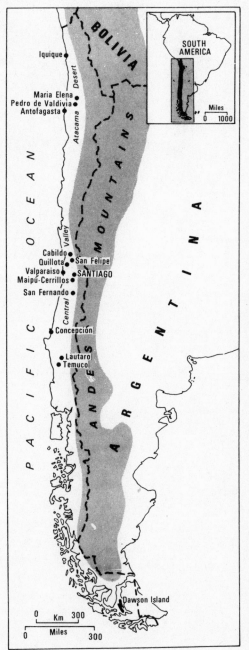

MAP OF CHILE

Showing localities mentioned in the text

My country has the shape of a great albatross with wings outspread!

And in that unforgettable meeting, in which we were striving to renegotiate our External Debt in a just fashion, many of those who appeared so implacable seemed to be taking aim in order to bring Chile tumbling down, so that the albatross should fly no more! To mention this may be the indiscretion of a poet who has only been an ambassador for a year, but it looked to me as though it was perhaps the representative of United States finance who concealed an arrow underneath his business papers — ready to aim it at the albatross's heart!

If he would take the trouble to reread the poets of former times, he might learn from *The Ancient Mariner* that the sailor who perpetrated such a crime was doomed to carry the heavy corpse of the slain albatross hanging from his neck — to all eternity.

PABLO NERUDA,
Nobel prize winner for poetry and Popular Unity ambassador to France, April 1972.

Introduction

Chile and the Popular Unity

Few foreigners knew much about Chile when, in September 1970, a Marxist president was elected. Yet the next three years were to make it a stage on which the world watched the re-enactment of almost all the classic problems of achieving socialism. In the last, bloody act, the name of Chile would be scored, like Spain's, across the minds of a generation.

The Popular Unity coalition supporting Salvador Allende with his programme for initiating a 'peaceful way toward socialism', won 36 per cent of the votes, against 34 per cent for the candidate of the right-wing National Party. Much propaganda was to be made of this lack of an overall majority. However, the Christian Democrats, who were previously in power under Eduardo Frei (1964-70) and won 28 per cent of the vote, had a programme almost as radical as the PU's, in the short term.

Following Allende's victory, capital was rushed out of the country. Congress, which was dominated by the opposition parties, still had to confirm the election result. It did so only after Allende had undertaken to 'respect the integrity' of the Church, the judiciary and the armed forces. Soon afterwards, the army's commander-in-chief, General Schneider, was assassinated. This turned out to have been an attempt by a small neo-fascist party, Fatherland and Freedom, to provoke military intervention. (It later emerged that the CIA was also involved.) The left, meanwhile, debated what all this meant for the future. It was in this climate that Allende took power on 3 November 1970.

The PU was a broad left coalition. Its largest components were the Communist and Socialist parties, which had combined in previous elections. The former, dating from the twenties, was traditionally committed to an electoral strategy. With its roots in the nitrate mines of the north, it was strongest among industrial workers. The Socialist Party was founded in 1933, by Allende among others. Though mostly Marxist, its followers ranged from Social Democrats to Trotskyists.

The Radicals and the MAPU (Movement of Popular United Action) were the coalition's junior partners. The Radicals were a long-standing social democratic party. Having led a Popular Front in the thirties, they dominated centrist politics until the newer Christian Democrats overtook them in the sixties. Their association with the PU provoked two splits, before and after 1970, further diminishing their numbers.

The MAPU was much the youngest party involved. Formed in 1969 by disillusioned Christian Democrats who adopted a Marxist position, it split twice in the PU period. First into the Christian Left, which dropped the explicitly Marxist label, but stayed in the PU and attracted more Christian Democrats; and later into the Workers' and Peasants' Movement (MOC). The latter was close to the Communist Party and also remained in the PU, making it finally a six-party coalition. The one substantial left-wing party outside it was the Revolutionary Left Movement (MIR). Cuban-influenced and of mainly student origin, it operated clandestinely until the PU's victory, then offered 'critical support' to Allende.

These parties naturally had differing views on Allende's accession in these turbulent circumstances. For the Communist Party, Radicals and many Socialists it vindicated the PU's premise: the strength of Chile's democratic traditions, even at moments of confrontation. For other Socialists and the MAPU and MIR, it had very different implications: that the Chilean ruling class would resort to violence when necessary.

The PU's philosophy was vague, though. In immediate terms it aspired only to establish the would-be preconditions for a transition to socialism. These included the nationalization of major resources and monopolies, both Chilean and foreign-owned; measures for workers' participation; and the completion and democratization of agrarian reforms already initiated by Frei. The question of how socialism would be finally achieved was left unstated.

In practice one sector of the PU saw armed confrontation with the right as inevitable. Another, led by Allende, felt that the left might win control, by gradual and constitutional means, of the entire state apparatus — the legislature and judiciary, still heavily controlled by the right, and the officially neutral armed forces. The latter, it was hoped, would at least divide in the event of a military coup, while victory in the congressional elections due in 1973 might pave the way for a Popular Assembly. This dominant, 'gradualist' position was particularly associated with the Communist Party. Both points of view were represented in the other PU parties, and it was precisely over these that the MAPU and the MOC were to finally split — the MOC to align with the 'gradualists', and the MAPU to join with the MIR, Christian Left and sections of the Socialist Party criticizing them as 'reformists'. Even in 1970, perhaps their one clear point of agreement was that the PU's victory was a critical step forward.

Three years later, on 11 September 1973, the armed forces overthrew the PU in a particularly violent coup, even for modern Latin America. President Allende died defiant in the burning Moneda Palace. United Nations sources estimate that thousands of his supporters were killed. A minority died fighting against clearly impossible odds. Others were publicly shot without trial, to create mass terror, in the factories, slums and rural communities sympathetic to the PU. Many are known to have died under torture. Thousands more were herded into gaols and concentration camps. The military junta under General Augusto Pinochet adopted a clearly fascist position: it suspended all human rights, banned political parties and trade unions, burned the electoral register and swore to 'eliminate Marxism' and 're-establish Western values'. It rapidly aligned with Brazilian-led ideological warfare on a continental scale, and established a terror apparatus that was to systematically destroy a generation of left-wingers.

Today, as the Chilean resistance develops, new forms of struggle have begun. Yet everywhere discussion of the PU continues, especially on the basic questions of the transition to socialism and relationships between left-wing parties. In Europe the 'lessons' of the Chilean coup are naturally felt to be crucial for the current strategies of the left.

Vital as this discussion is, it tends to ignore what happened in Chile *apart* from the coup. The Chilean experience is rarely examined, rather than used to vindicate predetermined positions. In practice the 'lessons' tend to be dogmas long pre-dating the PU. This also applies to much discussion among Chileans; but for others, such commentary neglects the concrete achievements in many fields by every group within the left, and their impact at a popular level.

Talking to Chilean exiles in Europe, we were immediately struck by this gulf between the concrete events and the pundits. Accounts of the PU period give little space to the views and experiences of those who were at the eye of the storm: the activists at the base of the parties. It was to these that we found ourselves talking about their work in the factories, farms and shantytowns in which dramatic changes occurred in 1970-3. Their experiences seemed more profound, and much more relevant to the future as accounts of the popular movement, than anything we had read on the subject. We noticed, though, that recollection of these experiences was fading. This was particularly poignant, since the PU's future history will depend heavily on oral records, given the coup's destructiveness and the left's own need to destroy information. It was this which led us to record and edit a selection of these activists' stories.

We have deliberately avoided offering our views on the 'lessons of Chile'. Our aim was to provide some answers to the question of a British docker involved in boycotting the junta, when he wondered aloud what he would have experienced, had he happened to be Chilean. We intervened little in the interviews. We have therefore felt free to omit our few questions. These simply asked for experiences of changes at a popular level and the speakers' understanding of them as members of particular parties. Interestingly, their activism involves much more than party lines. Individual creativity and political views are reciprocal forces. Even partisan interpretations do tend to be based on concrete experience, and hence on popular response as much as on any party doctrine.

The seven interviews selected are divided into four sections — industry, the countryside, the shantytowns and the universities. These are some of the major fronts on which PU activists were working. Each section has a purely informative introduction, and each speaker a short biographical note.

Common to all the interviews is a basically chronological structure, culminating with the coup. All of them refer to the impact of major political events, so we have compiled a chronology of the PU period. Together with the index, this should enable a comparison between the different ways in which these events and common themes are understood, according to the various speakers' fields and party affiliations.

The PU period can be divided into three phases. The first year is one of apparent successes: extensive nationalization, acceleration of land reform, a sharp reduction of unemployment, rising production and real wages and an outright majority for the PU in the municipal elections. The second phase, of roughly the PU's second year, is marked by growing polarization. On one side collaboration begins between the Christian Democrats and the solidly right-wing National Party, leading to the lorry-owners' strike in October 1972. On the other, new patterns of popular organization emerge, particularly the industrial cordons (*cordones industriales*) which developed in major cities (see chapters 2 and 3, especially). While the congressional elections showed that support for the PU was still growing, its final year was one of constant confrontation and mounting right-wing terrorism, as the military prepared to take action.

Each interview focuses on the field in which the speaker was most active. The number of interviews in each field reflects its relative importance: three for industry, two for the countryside and one each for the shantytowns and the universities. In the case of industry, anything less could scarcely have conveyed the range of views on its key issues, such as workers' participation: hence the three selected are from the Communist Party, the MAPU and the Socialist Party. The countryside posed a difficult choice, as this field is itself so varied. The two speakers we decided on are from the MAPU and the MOC. Since their split resulted precisely from the main debates within the PU, the speakers convey what these meant for the agrarian sector, in which the MAPU had always been strong. Each of the remaining sections is accounted for by a single speaker, from the MIR and the Communist Party respectively.

While we were anxious for an overall political balance, it was impossible to present each field from every party's point of view. Our selection was guided by the richness of the speakers' experience, rather than their affiliations. We should also make clear that they speak as members, but not as spokesmen, of their parties. Between them they certainly illustrate broadly the two main tendencies within the left, and their development through the period. The gradualist one of the Communist Party, Radicals, MOC and sectors of the Socialist Party saw the PU as the truest expression of the labour movement and all progressives: these should therefore support unreservedly its anti-imperialist, anti-monopolist position, which left the questions of state power and full socialism to a later stage. On the other hand the MAPU, Christian Left and the rest of the Socialists, together with the MIR, disputed that there could be two such 'stages'. The PU's commitment to legality and 'gradualism', involved it inevitably in compromises with the Chilean bourgeoisie. These checked the advance towards socialism and gave a free rein to right-wing subversion and its imperialist allies. The industrial cordons, *campesino* (peasants 'and rural workers')* councils and other popular organizations should actively oppose this trend with a vanguard 'popular power' of their own.

The 'gradualists' were not wholly denying the validity of the industrial cordons etc., any more than the others were suggesting abandoning the PU. The argument was essentially as to whether to support it unconditionally or critically: whether, given the mounting confrontation, it should 'consolidate' or 'advance'. However, as the polarization between the right and left gathered pace, this distinction grew increasingly urgent in ways apparent in every interview, especially as the coup starts looming.

There are perhaps two major themes in this polarization at the popular level. One is the struggle against the economic sabotage launched by the right; the other is the constant ideological confrontation, transforming people's consciousness at every turn. These processes are interwoven. New problems foster new awareness and new ways of dealing with them. The bourgeoisie's sabotage gave rise first to the local people's supply control committees (JAPs, *Juntas de Abastecimiento populares*), then to the industrial cordons and finally to the communal commands, combining workers.

*See Abbreviations and Glossary.

and *campesinos*. The ideological forging of the 'new man and woman' in Chile was inseparable from the everyday struggle to transform material conditions.

Finally we should mention briefly how the interviews were conducted. They all took place in 1974-5 in various European countries. They were in Spanish, tape-recorded, and followed no fixed formula. We usually held two interview sessions, lasting three or four hours in all. All the speakers were clearly informed of the exact nature of the project, and every effort has been made to preserve their anonymity and that of people to whom they referred. Even in exile their lives are not easy, while those of their comrades and relatives in Chile are much less so. We fully recognize and thank them for their confidence in us.

Few interviews are impersonal experiences. These were often intense and moving. The oldest person to whom we talked, a worker and long-standing unionist, was reluctant to tell his personal story, 'because in the struggle for socialism there aren't really individuals, only what people do together'. They bore this out still, in their lack of regret at the personal cost of their commitment. As individuals and as one people with a common goal — as we hope above all to have shown — we salute them.

C.H.
B.S.

PART I

THE INDUSTRIAL SECTOR

Background

Industrial workers in the mines and factories were the PU's key supporters, numerically and politically. Their particular history underlay the PU's formation and much of its political thinking. Their struggle began in the nitrate mines of northern Chile towards the end of the nineteenth century, when protests against starvation wages and working conditions produced the first working-class organizations. Most of these mines were foreign owned. This meant that for the working class the enemy was imperialism and its contradictions with national interests — a persistent distinction, central to PU strategy.

Out of these early organizations grew the first labour confederation and the Communist Party in the twenties, then in the thirties the Socialist Party. As described by Gregorio (ch. I), the atmosphere of the mining towns was one of systematic repression, a fertile ground for the emergent left-wing parties. Also constant fluctuations in the world demand for nitrate led to mass redundancies. These scattered the miners and spread their awareness throughout the length and breadth of Chile.

It was this labour movement's resurgence, after a period of repression, which forged the parties of the left into the Popular Front of the thirties. While dominated by the centrist Radical Party, this led to considerable state support for Chilean industrialization. Organizations like CORFO, the National Development Corporation, and interventionist legislation resulting from this period provided much of the legal basis for the PU's programme.

By the forties and fifties, this state support was going increasingly to the private rather than the public sector. Meanwhile foreign capital was concentrated in copper production. In the sixties, however, it dominated industrial growth. This entailed monopolistic, capital intensive enterprises which neither produced cheap popular goods nor increased industrial employment. Even in this 'modern' sector labour conditions remained repressive, as a means of attracting capital, as described by Roberto in chapter 2. In these circumstances the reformist image of the Christian Democrat Government waned. Protest increased from the labour movement, headed by the Communist-led CUT, the Central Workers Confederation. Attempts by the Christian Democrats to obstruct the trades-unions' growing power had little success. If anything they helped to motivate the labour movement's major part in reuniting the parties of the left in the PU coalition.

The PU's main proposal was to nationalize all basic resources and industrial monopolies, both foreign and nationally owned. Also legislation from the 1930s allowed for government take-overs ('interventions') in cases of mismanagement or insoluble labour disputes. This process, described by Gregorio who served as a government intervenor, led to further nationalization. The PU also committed itself to workers' participation in industry. As these three chapters will show, this was interpreted differently by the various PU parties. For Communist activists like Gregorio, it meant that workers should be consulted over the maintenance of production. For others, like Roberto, as a member of MAPU, and many Socialists such as Pablo (ch. 3), it meant workers actually deciding how the means of production should be utilized. There were, of course, variations within these two widely differing positions, and even within single parties, according to local circumstances.

These differences sprang from events as well as from pre-determined positions. The PU's first year brought unprecedented industrial growth. Wage increases and price controls increased buying power and hence demand: unemployment fell and popular living standards rose. For political and economic reasons this success was short-lived. Declining private investment was followed by production boycotts, lock-outs and even sabotage. The economy took a rapid downturn. The question of how to deal with this crisis divided the left, particularly after it came to a head in the 'bosses' strike' of October 1972, when private industry supported the stoppage by lorry-owners.

The PU leadership stressed the importance of maintaining production and played down the mounting class confrontation, which it considered premature. This position was criticized by the MAPU, many Socialists and the MIR. Instead they demanded official support for workers' factory occupations with a view to government intervention, and also for the industrial cordons. These associations of workers in neighbouring factories arose mainly in response to the boycott and especially to the bosses' strike. Beginning in Santiago, Valparaiso and Concepción, they spread to other major cities and became increasingly organized. The PU leadership recognized these organizations, but felt that devolving power to them would antagonize the right much more than it would strengthen the left. At stake was its basic strategy of not alienating the middle sectors. Also at issue was the extent to which the cordons acknowledged or were felt to supersede the CUT's (and hence also the Communist Party's) traditional control of the labour movement. Especially in areas where cordons expanded into communal commands incorporating *campesinos*, students and non-industrial workers, this meant a widening gap between the PU's leadership and its base. The extent of this gap was a matter of opinion; particularly party opinion, as is evident in Gregorio's views as compared to those of Roberto and Pablo.

Gregorio, with his deep experience of the labour movement's history, defends the PU's position as fundamentally realistic. Roberto argues quite differently from the viewpoint of his work as a full-time unionist in Valparaiso and Santiago: workers were ready for the advances which the situation demanded. This is also Pablo's position, in the context of a single industrial cordon, and its development into the communal command of Maipú-Cerrillos in Santiago.

Each speaker bases his case on concrete local variations: the advanced and concentrated awareness of Santiago's working class, as against the relative isolation of workers in smaller plants like Gregorio's. Ultimately, though, the debate is clearly on a strategic level. Whether experience has brought it closer to agreement can perhaps be surmised from the conclusions which each of these speakers draws for the future.

1
The Chilean Way to Socialism: from company town to a nationalized copper industry

Speaker: GREGORIO, 47, member of the Communist party and mining technician employed by ENAMI (The National Mining Enterprise) as 'intervenor,' or interim manager, of several small copper plants subject to Government intervention

Growing up in the mining regions: the roots of the Chilean labour movement

I never knew my mother and father. They died soon after I was born. My father worked on the railways and was killed in a railway accident when he was only twenty-four. My mother followed him a year later. I was brought up by my grandparents. My grandfather worked in a copper mine in Potrerillos, in northern Chile. A few years later we moved further north to the nitrate zone, to Maria Elena, a mining town near Antofagasta. This was in the thirties, times were hard. My grandfather worked in the nitrate mine and I helped out to make ends meet. I ran errands and polished shoes, doing what I could for a few escudos. Maria Elena was a company town, the nitrate mine was German-Chilean and most of the managers were foreign. I'd make a bit extra by ball-boying on tennis courts in the management compound. Sometimes I gardened for them too. My grandparents were careful to send me to school at an early age, but even so I carried on working.

My grandfather belonged to the Communist Party. From as early as I can remember he'd explain to me what this meant, and the workers' hopes for a better future. In those days in the nitrate zone all left-wing politics were clandestine. The bosses forbade political meetings and visits by the workers' leaders who travelled round organizing the struggle for better wages and working conditions and for freedom of expression.

Most nitrate workers were aware of these things, though. It was they who'd launched this struggle. One of my earliest memories is of my grandfather bringing home strangers at night. Or I'd wake up to find them sleeping there —clandestine labour organizers. Often their visits coincided with a strike in the mine, and my grandfather would explain it to me — why they were striking and why their leaders had to come secretly, at night. Seeing how they were hounded taught me what workers were up against in their struggle for justice. I never forgot this, in spite of my later going on to get a technical education and with it certain privileges.

All of us kids in the nitrate zone learnt such things one way or another. Most parents made a point of taking us to political meetings. Their being forbidden only added to the excitement. They were out in the desert after dark. Though the days in the north are burning hot, the night is usually bitterly cold. We'd be wrapped up in our ponchos, people would bring food to share. They wasted no time — the meetings began as soon as everyone was there as there was always a fair chance that the police would break them up. Sometimes the bosses knew, and ignored them, but when someone well known was due to speak they'd usually send the police along. Often there'd be a ding-dong battle. Quite a few times I had to leg it along the gullies, tripping over and getting home all out of breath. I didn't think much of it at the time.

The nitrate mines are open cast and working conditions

in them were terrible — the heat and the dust. Although the
workers were starting to talk of an eight-hour day, this was
only a hope for the future. The shift was still from dawn to
dusk. The company fixed the hours and the workers had no
choice. Wages were hardly enough to live on and partly paid
in tallies which could be spent only at the company store,
the *pulperia*. The company controlled everything, housing,
water, electricity. The lights came on at eight o'clock, and
at eleven they turned them off — after that we weren't even
allowed to keep a lamp burning in the workers' compound
without permission. The water came on for a few hours
daily, you had to queue up at the tap for it and keep it in
tins. The store was like a fortress. You couldn't go in without
the company's identity card, and both the doors were
guarded by dogs, big German boxers. The officials would
watch your every move. They were mostly young English-
men and Germans. You handed over your tally and they'd
give you your ration — a kilo of sugar, flour, two kilos of
potatoes. Then as you went out through the turnstile they'd
check through everything you had. If they held you up, the
dogs would try and get at you.

There were different schools and housing areas. One
school for the managers' kids, where they taught mostly in
English and German — even the teachers were foreign.
Then there was another for the technicians' children, and a
state school for the mob, like myself. In ours we had only the
vaguest idea of what went on in the other two, of the games
they played, for example. The workers' houses belonged to
the company, and the rent was deducted from wages. They
all had two rooms and corrugated iron roofs, like ovens in
the day and freezers at night. The technicians lived in a
separate compound in proper brick houses with tiled roofs.
Finally there was the management compound, where the
foreigners lived in big bungalows with gardens and lawns,
all carefully fenced.

Workers couldn't organize openly. Where the union
existed, it was only in name. The most effective organizers

were those who'd worked outside the community, gaining experience which they passed on. Political pamphlets and papers were forbidden, they had to be smuggled in. This was my first political task — I and other kids would bring them in under our jackets a few at a time and distribute them. At our age we weren't suspected. In these ways workers gradually became more aware of their conditions, and strikes and protests began to increase. The company's policy was to sack anyone involved and turn them out of their rented houses; if the police wouldn't do this for them, they'd use their own security forces. Confrontations began to increase. On several occasions workers were killed, both in Maria Elena and in the neighbouring nitrate town of Pedro de Valdivia.

Although my grandfather explained everything to me, he never directly tried to persuade me to join the youth section of the Communist Party. When I said I wanted to join, he said: 'Fine, but make sure it's your own decision.' This meant it was a firm one. After joining I learnt a lot more from the local youth-section organizer. His way of opening our eyes was to have us read both party papers and those of the official press and judge for ourselves where the real truth lay. With the world we lived in, that wasn't hard.

By thirteen I'd finished primary school. As I'd done well, I got a job as an office boy with the nitrate company in Pedro de Valdivia. As luck would have it my boss there was different from the others. He encouraged me to get a technical training. Eventually I managed to go to the technical school in Antofagasta, where I studied engineering.

This was the time of the *Ley Maldita*, the 'infamous law' of the late 1940s, which banned the Communist Party. Left-wing workers were rounded up in the mining areas and shipped off to labour camps. When they left on the train, their relatives gathered at the station, and they'd go off singing to keep up their spirits. The favourite song was the tango *Adios Pampa Mia*. Somehow my grandfather wasn't detained, but one of my uncles was shipped out. Like many others, he escaped and went underground in Antofagasta, with the protection of the Party. As I was studying there, I was in contact with him and with the labour movement. The Party was especially strong among the dockers in Antofagasta — my uncle got work there in the docks, but like my father he was killed in a working accident.

Quite a few of us students at the technical college were in the Party. Of course, we had to keep this quiet, but we organized ourselves round the questions of better grants for technical students and the founding of a technical university. We were all very badly off — wealthy families looked down on technical training. I paid my way through with vacation work in Pedro de Valdivia. Later I also had a small scholarship from the nitrate workers' union. I wrote to them once to tell them how my studies were going, and the letter was read out at a meeting. My grandfather told me how pleased they all were. This sort of thing was the beginning of growing contacts between workers, students and professionals which were later to be crucial. My fellow students were of similar background, hence our firmness on the question of grants and the technical university. Although the police broke up most of our meetings, we stuck to these issues. Eventually our pressures led to the founding of the Technical University in Santiago — and to its being a left-wing stronghold.

After my studies in Antofagasta I applied to the military academy, but with little chance of getting in. To do so you virtually had to have been to university and have the right political connections. This is why the Chilean officer corps is so very upper-class to this day, and largely from Anglo or German-Chilean families. Soon after this, though, the Technical University was founded in Santiago, and I enrolled there. But ironically I and many others couldn't afford to complete our studies. After a year I had to give up and return to the North.

For fifteen years I worked my way up in the nitrate industry as a technician. This set me apart from the workers in terms of salary and living conditions, but as a member of the Party I did my best to support the workers whenever a dispute occurred. Many other technicians with a similar background did the same, and we were in a strong position, because the firms couldn't do without us. They'd often replace us with technicians from the South, but they didn't know the machinery as we did. Also the workers would support us by striking over a technician's dismissal, if it were for political reasons. This gave us the strength to back their claims for better conditions and wages etc.

This came to a head for me in the sixties, when the company for which I was working had a productivity drive. In some sections this meant mechanization and many workers lost their jobs. In others, mine included, the firm demanded increased output. We managed this, but when the workers demanded a corresponding rise, the management said they couldn't afford it. So they struck. I backed them — I was doubly angry because I'd been used to increase the workers' exploitation. I was no stooge. Well, this turned the heat on me. The boss dressed me down in front of the workers. So I said that unless their demands were met, I'd quit the job. They weren't, so I did so. Afterwards the management begged me to stay. They offered me all sorts of incentives, a salary increase and a new house, but I'd had enough. I'd been caught for too long between my own past and the privileges I'd obtained. I decided to leave the nitrate zone and look for employment further south.

This was how I came to be working in the copper industry in the late sixties, in the central province of Aconcagua. Apart from the big copper companies there were also some smaller private ones coordinated by ENAMI, the National Mining Enterprise, which provides them with credits and technical assistance. With my qualifications I managed to get a job with ENAMI, and went as technical supervisor to a copper plant in the town of Cabildo.

A measured victory: the electoral campaign in Aconcagua

It was here that I participated in the campaign of 1970. This reinforced my conviction that the PU's programme for the 'Chilean way to socialism' was fundamentally realistic. The obstacles I encountered confirmed the need to work within existing legal institutions. Aconcagua's economy is a mixture of mining and agriculture. Its small copper concerns, with anything from twenty to two hundred workers, are isolated from one another and generally far from the nearest large town. The workers tend to visit it about once a month, sometimes less often. This meant political isolation.

The plant in which I worked refined copper from many scattered mines. Some were nearby, with their workers living in Cabildo, but others were right up in the Andes, a hundred kilometres away : their workers came there only rarely. On the other hand those in Cabildo had good conditions compared to those in the nitrate zone. Housing was cheap and reasonable, and the plant was one of the most modern in Chile. I was there when it was inaugurated by Frei. They laid on a real ceremony. ENAMI was controlled from top to bottom by Christian Democrats, and they made the most of such occasions. More importantly, all this meant that most of the workers were Christian Democrat supporters — they had to be, to get a job there. This was also true of the countryside — the *campesinos* were also very isolated and seduced by the promise of land reforms. In short the opposition was strong, even at a popular level. Frei's promises were wearing thin, but not everywhere. We had to tread carefully.

Besides, even those who were disillusioned had somehow to be assured that the PU wasn't just making promises like the governments before it. So we concentrated our campaign on the programme's most immediate aspects. I attended countless union meetings to put across our proposals for improved housing, work security, and better education, for instance, We distributed the PU's literature, and listened to people's questions and doubts. When these were raised we'd consult with the leadership and try to bring back concrete answers.

Certainly the PU parties increased their vote in the area, but only on a modest scale. There wasn't that feeling that the tide was turning, which people seemed to have had elsewhere, especially in Santiago. When we learnt the national results, there was singing and dancing in the streets, but it was muted. We were well aware that although the PU had won, it was only on a minority vote, that the way ahead was far from easy. Such considerations weighed heavily on most of us in the Communist Party when we came to implementing the programme.

Implementing the PU programme: participation and the maintenance of production

ENAMI had a number of roles. Its basic one was to help to maintain the level of production on which the PU's success, to our way of thinking, largely depended. This also meant an increasing number of interventions in plants with financial or labour problems. Finally, like other state agencies, it had to realize the PU's programme for workers' participation in management.

I became deeply involved in these issues, because soon after the elections I was appointed as 'intervenor' to a copper plant in difficulties, and subsequently to another. The first case was straightforward. A smallish plant in Aconcagua had failed to meet its obligations to improve both wages and working conditions. The workers finally struck, called off their negotiations with the owners, and demanded government intervention. The Minister of Labour went into this and then agreed. I was appointed for my combination of technical know-how with sympathy for the PU's objectives.

My first job was to go to the plant and hear both sides of

the argument, from the owners and workers. After that I had to make an economic and social assessment, and finally provide some recommendations. As it turned out, both sides had a case. The plant was heavily in debt and outdated and there was a backlog of unpaid wages. Nothing could be done to save it, so in the end my task was simply to wind it up and find alternative jobs for the workers. With the PU's success in increasing growth and hence employment, this wasn't hard. Within a few months it was all sorted out and everyone was satisfied — the Ministry of Labour, ENAMI, the workers and even the owners.

In the following year I was called on again as intervenor for a small copper plant. This was was much more complicated, and lasted right up to the military coup. It involved all the PU's major concerns: the need to avoid class confrontations, to keep production up to the mark and to involve the workers themselves in what the PU was doing.

The first difficulty lay in people's different expectations of an official intervention. The owners were often glad of it, imagining that the intervenor would simply arrive with a fistful of money and make no fundamental changes. On the other hand, sections of the left were for immediate nationalization and virtual control by the workers themselves. In fact intervention was not a commitment to either of these two positions. The government was a popular one, but its targets for nationalization were the big monopolies only. The ultra-left's insistence on pushing it much further and deeper caused economic and political problems. For one thing there had to be good reason for intervening in the first place, in order to be within the law and avoid alarming the middle classes — which also meant consultation with the owners and reasonable compensation. Also the government then had to maintain such industries: it wasn't practical to expropriate left, right and centre, as certain sectors were demanding. Our main focus was on the strategic concerns, which the government needed to control. With these controversies, an intervenor was virtually walking a tightrope.

On relationships with the owners, my party's position was quite clear. While our concern was for workers' interests, we weren't seeking confrontations. Whatever the outcome of intervention, it should be on a legal basis. This reflected the PU's strategy of sticking strictly to legal methods. Without this, we'd have lost our main strength as a legally elected government, with support from all progressive sectors. This wasn't a 'non-working class' position. It was often repeated by Figueroa, the president of the CUT, for instance. So I had to try and get on with the owners — though in the end it proved impossible — in order to keep the factory working. My main contact at first was with the shopfloor's PU committee, and although this tended to divide, I always consulted very closely with workers who belonged to the Party. But at the same time, I had to keep the owners informed of my decisions and intentions.

There'd been problems in this plant for years. It was a good way from Cabildo itself and very much a family firm. The manager was the owner's son, the local mayor was a relative, in short the family ran the area. The plant smelted copper from several small mines, the biggest of which belonged to the firm and was right nearby. About 130 people worked in the plant and mine together. Again the intervention arose from a strike provoked by the owners' failure to implement an agreement on wages, working conditions and so on.

My impartiality upset the owners. As soon as they realized I wasn't there at their convenience, and that I also consulted the workers, they turned nasty. The owner's son, the manager, was constantly creating problems. For instance he'd tell me there was some snag which I'd then have to go and deal with, only to find that he'd invented it. The main trouble was that there was also a 'yellow' (boss's) section of the union which he controlled, consisting of the technicians and a few of the manual workers. They were always making trouble with the others — the majority, whose strike had led to the intervention. One day this provoked a fight between them. I found it had been instigated by one of the yellow union workers and asked the manager to dismiss him. He refused, so I sent him an order in writing, but he still refused, so I demoted him. Then he threatened to resign, and the yellow union supported the charge that I'd victimized him — they were thirty men in all, less than a quarter of the total. Well, I let him go, and most of his supporters went with him. Some came back, but it caused problems. For one thing his family got the local press to denounce us. They also brought a lawsuit against me. More importantly, we were left almost without technicians.

This was serious, given the importance of maintaining production. Our only way out was for all of us to discuss it together. This meant in effect that we introduced workers' participation before we otherwise would have done. The nature of this participation was much debated within the left, but in our case the reason for it was clear — as I said, it was the only way to maintain production in the circumstances. I was responsible for implementing it, and this was the way I put it across: to keep the plant running, all of us had to participate in our different ways at every level in making the necessary decisions and taking responsibility for them. We followed the government's blueprint for this. There was a General Administrative Council (*Consejo General de Administración*), consisting of myself as intervenor and two union representatives, one manual, the other a white-collar worker. There was also a Technical Administrative Council (*Consejo Técnico de Administración*) with a delegate from each section — one from maintenance, one from transport, one from processing, etc. Each delegate was elected by a secret ballot in union meetings. Finally there was the General Assembly (*Asamblea*) of all the workers in the plant. All my decisions were referred to it, on accounts, production schedules and so forth. There were also Production Committees (*Comités de Producción*) in each section, to ensure that they were keeping to schedule.

The workers' response soon compensated for the loss of

the technicians. Many of the more experienced men were capable of replacing them. But I still stressed that responsibility should depend on experience and qualifications. The workers' views should be respected, but important decisions still had to be taken by those qualified to take them. While the workers should participate, this participation had its limits: they weren't equipped to take managerial decisions. In our case this wasn't much disputed, but I know that elsewhere the official scheme for participation was criticized by other left parties as technocratic. But how else could we maintain production, as the PU required of us? This was a technical problem and we treated it as such. And we succeeded in maintaining production. Governing was the government's job. Ours was to support it as it required.

Besides, when workers were allowed to take all the decisions, this encouraged self-interestedness. They often demanded wage increases instead of further productive investments, and the Christian Democrats used this to divide the workers and cause stoppages. I remembered their strength in the first copper plant I worked in — this too was good reason for limiting participation to the PU's formula for it. And it worked. There was little dissension, and the assembly dealt mainly with the workers' immediate concerns: wages, housing, sanitary conditions in the plant, etc. As a result, we paid our way without any need for government subsidies. This was my main goal, and we achieved it.

Unequal odds: the approach of the coup

Of course when the boycott of the economy by the private sector began, it was hard to keep production up. The first lorry-owners' strike in October 1972 didn't affect us as much as elsewhere, as we had a reserve of raw materials. This was true of the zone as a whole. Food supplies weren't a serious problem, with its being an agricultural area. The only real one was transport. The union helped to solve this by using our trucks to market the *campesinos'* products. The workers drove them on a voluntary basis. The far-right wasn't well organized yet, so we met with little opposition.

In the following year's tank revolt (*tancazo*) in June, the workers showed their determination by immediately report-ing to the factory, ready to defend it at any cost. But it was over on the same day, and things were rapidly back to normal. At the time some of the workers did ask why the PU didn't get tough with the military, instead of negotiating with them. I had to talk to them, to explain the government's position, that it was trying to avoid a confrontation; that we should have faith in our leaders' attempts to find a just and effective solution, and that they needed our support. The workers did feel in the end that this was where the answer lay. They never lost their confidence that if there was a way out of the crisis, the PU leaders would find it. They listened to Allende's speech immediately after the *tancazo* and followed his request to go back to normal work and redouble their efforts for the PU.

We had no local industrial cordon, as there was little industry, so the union dealt with these issues. But in the tank coup, as in the first bosses' strike, the workers combined with the *campesinos*. Together they set up road blocks and took other defensive measures. This showed their determi-nation to defend the government, and was a warning to the right. As a result its second strike was much more organized and violent. The lorry-owners now intervened against our trucks which were maintaining food distribution. Although they sometimes came off worse, they usually had the upper hand, as they were often armed and we weren't. Some of the workers wanted to commandeer the owners' trucks — but we hadn't the means to take them over, as they were all parked together and defended by the police.

They never gave up the struggle, though. By this time we were having problems with parts, as we couldn't get them from Santiago, but the workers often found solutions. The older ones had been in the industry so long that they could improvise most parts. They also had relatives and friends who were old hands at this sort of thing. We discussed these problems in the assembly, and one of them would say: 'I know just the man for the job, up north.' A few days later he'd be there, with the parts or some means of fixing them. In a way, they were our best times, with everyone pooling all their talents and determined not to be defeated. If anything, their confidence in the PU was higher than ever.

The fact was, though, that we were up against fascism. We had no means to defend ourselves against the right's methods. Just before the coup, I had orders which must have originated with the military, to give full details on all the workers — which of them had done military service, where and when, and so on. Another order demanded full details of all the dynamite used in the mine, when we were due to get new supplies, where they were coming from etc. Eventually they were severely restricted. By the time of the coup we were down to eight sticks of dynamite.

On 11 September I was in Santiago — I'd gone there to consult with ENAMI over some administrative problems. Early in the morning I heard the planes passing over the city, and then the thuds as they bombed the Presidential Palace. I listened to the commentary on the truck radio and realized what was happening. When I tried to get into ENAMI it was already full of soldiers. They wouldn't admit me. I tried to make contact with the Party, but that was also impossible, so I headed back to Cabildo.

When I got there, other party members were still waiting for instructions. We never received them, and later realized that the regional committee had been cut off. The plant was occupied by the military. There was nothing I could do. As my name had been broadcast as one of those required to report to the new authorities, I did so. They let me go free, but the next morning they came to arrest me. The former owner of the plant had charged me with being a subversive.

I was gaoled, beaten about a bit and tried in a military court, but as there was no evidence against me, the case was finally dismissed. But of course I was sacked and blacklisted. I tried getting odd jobs here and there, but with a family to support I couldn't manage, so I had to leave Chile.

Looking back, I feel that the PU did all it could to save the day. I still think that the odds were too heavily against us, that we weren't ready to take them on if it came to a final confrontation. It wasn't just a defeat, because a fifty-year-long struggle can't be wiped out by a military coup. Today the popular forces have even wider support than they did, from people who've learnt what fascism is. I know we'll come back into our own and stronger than before. If there were mistakes it wasn't these, but fascism, that overthrew the PU. What matters is the people's awareness. And this is measured not by mistakes, but by their will and experiences.

2

The Working Class and the Struggle for Power: from workers' participation to the communal commands

Speaker: ROBERTO, 40, activist of the MAPU and full-time trade-union organizer, who worked during the PU in the major industrial areas of Santiago and Valparaiso

A factory worker's experiences: the force behind the PU

I joined the union when I was fifteen — the Shoeworkers' Federation. I was working in a factory in Santiago. Three years later I was branch secretary. Experience taught me early on that it was only by uniting that we could defend our interests as workers. For instance in our biggest strike, when we occupied the factory for weeks, it was other workers living round it who saw us through. They fought pitched battles with the police to get food and blankets to us. Workers have few resources. We have to pool them and pull together. Ever since recognizing this I've tried to base my actions on it. That's why I'm in exile today on the instructions of my party.

I worked in this factory for eighteen years, and left when I was thirty-three, after one of our regular showdowns. The management bought new machinery, but not to raise output. Instead they made half the workers redundant, men with up to forty years of service. They'd never get another job, and the compensation was a pittance. I protested but to my disgust my fellow unionists wouldn't support me. This was under Frei, when crises of this kind were common and resistance brought retaliation. Their argument was: we can only defend our working conditions — hiring and firing is the boss's prerogative. I was so fed up that I almost came to blows with my colleagues. In the end I decided to leave the factory.

I set up shop as a cobbler in the shantytown where we were living, on the outskirts of Santiago. We had a house lot there and built our own home. The floor was bare earth and the roof was made of hardboard, but I was happy. I had no boss, and I was politically active in my neighbourhood association, which we set up to defend our own interests. But I couldn't forget what had happened in the factory. I realized that although the union defended the workers' immediate interests, it could never change relations between the exploiters and the exploited. The bosses had done as they pleased with the men — and once you're out of work in Chile, there's no unemployment benefit and ten applicants for every job. You take what they give you.

All this time I'd had no connection with any political party. Then I came into contact with some young people working in a literacy programme. They were using the methods of Paulo Freire, which include the raising of political awareness. One day I heard Freire speak, and we got into a debate — I felt he was overlooking things which were important to factory workers. Later we came to know one another, and this got me reading seriously. Marx, especially. It wasn't easy, but what gripped me was how it explained my own experience. The reading was a real struggle though. Some nights I'd sleep only two or three hours, I'd read and read, and even so I might cover only twenty pages — I was determined to take it all in. I'd left school at twelve, you see, and although I'd learnt to read and write I was functionally illiterate. Like most Chileans I'd had nothing to read.

Meantime I enrolled in an adult education course, to

complete my secondary school training. I finished this inside
a year. From then on I spent all my free time organizing
young people's cultural centres in my own and other
shantytowns. I kept stressing that young people's problems
could be understood and dealt with only in terms of their
class situation. All our discussions came back to the point. In
the end we set up a federation of four hundred cultural
centres.

In 1969 the MAPU was formed. I and many other
comrades from the cultural centres joined the party. Most of
the others had been Christian Democrats. I was assigned to
the party's mass front, to develop educational programmes
for unionists and factory workers.

From unionist to party activist: workers' education courses

Through the party I was sent to Valparaiso to teach in an
extension programme for workers run by the Catholic
University. The course was vocational, but we gave it a
political perspective. We included the history of the labour
movement. For instance we showed how the labour laws had
developed to control the unions. We also discussed where
different parties stood on these questions. This projected the
PU's programme right into the unions and factories, and
aroused discussion of its proposals throughout the campaign
of 1970. This was crucial. Chilean workers have a great
respect for education, and now they really had the chance to
focus it on their own situation.

With the PU in power, our discussions turned to the
problems of implementing the programme. Our main
concern was with the scope for workers' own initiatives in
pressing their proposals home, especially those for nationalization and for workers' participation. We took our course
right into the factories in the Valparaiso area. Many of these
were subsequently taken over by the workers, and then
transferred to public ownership. One typical case was a
cement factory in a small town called La Calera. It was

almost the only local employment, which gave it an iron grip on its workers — if they were sacked, they'd have to leave home to look for a job. So they were completely cowed by their bosses — the wages and working conditions were terrible. But after we held a summer school there, in which all this company's workers took part, its power crumbled. A union was formed, and this produced a confrontation and occupation of the factory. The government intervened and eventually nationalized it. It became a model of increasing workers' participation and finally of workers' control.

My own experience as a worker came in handy on these courses. I didn't use texts to convey our message, but popular images. For better or worse, I'd even turn to the *machismo* common among Chilean workers. 'Now, comrade' — this would be a in a group discussion — 'supposing your wife has another man, and you find out — what happens then?' 'What happens? We fix him.' 'Right then, society includes exploiters and the exploited. You find this out — what happens then?' 'What happens? We fix the exploiters — no more bosses.' Later our discussions would move on to workers' participation, its different forms, its real purpose. They'd give examples of what was happening in their own factories. We'd deal with everything in class terms, but always through the workers' own imagery and in terms of their own experience.

Workers' initiatives: expropriations and new forms of participation

For the next three years I continued working for the party's mass front on union affairs in Santiago and Valparaiso. One of the most important aspects of the PU process, as we in the MAPU understood it, was workers' participation. All sectors of the left acknowledged this, but they understood it in different ways. Some saw it only as a basic support for PU's economic measures: but our view was that it should lead to workers' control, as an antidote to the bureaucracy. In practice, though, it wasn't we activists who made the decisions, it was the workers. Their new awareness and initiatives came from experience, not theories — particularly from the crisis produced by the factory-owners' boycott, when they started cutting investments. This crisis became so acute that the workers had to find answers to it.

Their first answer was to occupy factories which were sabotaging production. This enabled them to maintain the factory and ask for government intervention. Of course it raised the most basic question — the ownership of the means of production — but as I say, this was in response to the day-to-day needs of the struggle in progress. In Santiago alone, over three hundred factories became subject to government intervention, and most of these were outside the PU's original programme. This had provided for nationalizing only the biggest, monopolistic concerns, about 150 in all. But we saw this as a false distinction. We stressed that the prospect of socialism divides loyalties along class lines — that the bourgeoisie as a whole would resist, which meant a need for popular power, working-class organizations within the shell of the bourgeois State. Only these could guarantee the PU's advances. In taking this position, though, we were responding mainly to workers' initiatives — steps they took because they were closest to the development of the conflict.

This shows that a revolutionary process is never something deriving from textbooks. New situations have to be dealt with and this produces new ways forward. For example, when food supplies were short, the working-class neighbourhoods set up JAPs, people's supply control committees, which not only limited speculation — they also compelled many middle-class people who couldn't afford black-market prices to accept their basic principle of equal shares at official prices. Sometimes they even helped to organize them, under working-class direction. In this way they were drawn into the workers' battle — and on workers' terms — against the bourgeoisie's manoeuvres, because only the workers could counteract them.

I could cite more examples of how these concrete developments made the workers their own vanguard, because they're the ones who control production. It was they who gave meaning to the PU's measures — the PU itself was too heterogeneous to respond to the changes which it set in motion. Officially, expropriation depended on a decision from above. But in practice we had to fight from below, not only for its implementation, but for its results to be effective as a product of class struggle.

We set about this in the following way. Taking a particular area, we'd find out which factories had been involved in the most disputes, which were best organized politically, and whether the owners were reducing or even sabotaging production. On this basis we'd select one for an agitational programme. Activists would distribute pamphlets and bulletins throughout the area, especially at factory gates. This made other workers aware of the issue. Meantime the party would strengthen contacts inside the factory, raising the possibility of the workers requesting intervention and eventually expropriation. These projects had to be carefully planned. Spontaneity meant the risk of serious setbacks. Party discipline at the base is crucial in these situations.

Often, though, these demands were spontaneous, in which case we mobilized support from workers in the neighbouring factories. But either way they were often at odds with PU policy. One such case was the Rayon-Said factory. With a labour force of about two thousand, and a near monopoly of rayon and cellophane production, it should have been due for nationalization, but in fact the government was against this. It had an unofficial agreement with the factory owner, the magnate Said, who also owned the *Banco del Trabajo*, one of the biggest private banks. In return for its nationalization — together with the whole banking system — the PU had undertaken to leave the Rayon factory alone. So the workers took the initiative —

and they did so consciously in answer to this compromise by their government. They demanded a rise, which wasn't given, then occupied the factory in order to get it expropriated. They had a long struggle, but they succeeded. More than succeeded — they got the support of the workers in another Said monopoly and later this too was taken over. During the factory occupation they also got help, both food and money, from the nearby *campesinos*, as many of themselves were *ex-campesinos*, an important factor in building this alliance. After the expropriation, they had training to enable them to manage the factory independently.

We had experiences like this throughout the province of Valparaiso. The main textile factory in Viña del Mar would probably not have been taken over but for pressure from the workers. They'd been fighting a reactionary management for years. Under Frei they struck for six months to get it turned into a cooperative. This failed and half the workers were dismissed. They tried and failed again, with a further month's strike, in Frei's last year. More 'temporary' dismissals were threatened in order to modernize the factory but the workers wouldn't have this, knowing they'd never get their jobs back. The argument was still going on when the PU was elected, but even it was non-committal. So the factory was occupied again. This time the workers refused to leave until it was expropriated, against the original decision of the Minister of Economics.

These struggles created a powerful base to build on after expropriation. This textile factory in Viña del Mar wasn't only transferred to the public sector, but came to be fully controlled by its workers. They decided to reorganize its production and distribution patterns. They designed cheaper, more popular materials, and started distributing them through the JAPs and other popular organizations with their rationing and price controls. In this way the whole process was socialized, right from production to consumption. These experiments dealt crippling blows to the capitalist system, built as they were on the workers' growing recognition that they couldn't change their part of it without transforming it as a whole.

Officially workers' participation was much more limited and formal. Production committees were appointed for each section of the factory, from among the trade-union officials — one for the administrative section, another for the mechanics and so on, depending on the number of sections. The heads of these production committees and other union officials then elected five members of the General Administrative Council. This was the main managing body, to which the government appointed five more representatives, plus a director — six in all. So even at plant level the bureaucrats were in the majority, as well as controlling the higher levels of economic decision making.

In practice then, workers still had no power to amend production schedules etc., let alone initiate them. This provoked a lot of discussion, especially among workers in the big metallurgical and textile concerns in the public sector. They argued that government nominees on the administrative councils should also be workers from the factory, since this was a workers' government. It was pointed out that under the official system the technocrats were the majority, whereas the workers were concerned with the social aspects of production. In one large factory called Solimar, producing boilers and railway engines, the workers actually struck on this issue. Eventually they won their case and made a thorough-going revision of every aspect of production. Working conditions were improved, excess technicians were transferred and wage differentials were reduced. Through voluntary overtime, production was raised sufficiently to cancel the company's outstanding debt. Despite their lack of management training the workers themselves reorganized things from start to finish.

It was argued that these changes would destabilize production — but far from this happening, it was in sectors where participation was weakest that there was real instability. In copper, for instance. Officials in this sector refused to contemplate real changes, because it's such a vital export. So what happened after its nationalization? The workers regarded the State like a traditional employer, and demanded wage increases way above the rate of inflation, even in 1973, when the economy was in crisis. The government refused, and right-wing, white-collar and higher-skilled workers saw their chance and carried other workers with them. And of course the right-wing parties supported them, financially and with their propaganda. The government had to give in, and its whole wage policy collapsed.

This could never have happened if there'd been effective participation in this sector. As in the case of the Solimar factory the PU failed to understand that the ideological battleground was among the working class itself, not just among the 'middle sectors': that its loyalty could be held only by giving it a real role in the process of building socialism. Without this it could at best be passive, and at worst manipulated.

The industrial cordons, the bosses' strikes and the rise of the communal commands

It was out of these actions by vanguard workers that the industrial cordons developed. What crystallized them was cooperation between the workers of different factories to counteract the 'bosses' strike' of October 1972, which would otherwise have halted production. Afterwards they continued expanding right up to the time of the coup. The workers realized that the stoppage was no isolated event, but part of a struggle ultimately for control of the means of production. The cordons were both a defence measure and a step in this direction, an embryo of popular power. The PU did recognize them, but only in the restricted role of defending the government on its own terms — while much of the union hierarchy opposed them. Their real basis was in the working class itself, in the face of a daily mounting conflict. This was the most important effect of real workers' participation, especially in state-owned enterprises. These were the vanguard of the cordons, and as such the seeds of the revolution, which participation germinated.

The debate on popular power began soon after Allende's election. The more radical parties — MAPU, MIR and the left wing of the Socialist Party — envisaged Cuban-style 'committees for the defence of the revolution', one in every neighbourhood. But this was utopian. Our problem wasn't one of defending an established socialism, but rather of countering attacks on our limited advances towards it, especially in the factories. From the outset the right campaigned ferociously against the PU's nationalizations. In Congress it obstructed them and starved the government of funds to run the nationalized concerns. In the courts it tried to declare them illegal. In the media, still largely controlled by the right, it swore to Chile and all the world that state-owned industries couldn't work — which it was already trying to ensure by sabotage and boycotts in the private sector. The right even tried to enlist the workers. At which point their lack of participation became a really critical weakness. Alienation made them prey to sophisticated propaganda which identified the managers in the public sector as the 'new bosses'. Many workers were saying as much, because in the circumstances there was some truth in it. They were being asked to produce more, on the grounds that the factories belonged to the workers — but this was contradicted by the lack of real participation.

Their disenchantment reached such a pitch that the right-wing's accusations came true — state-owned enterprises began to run into real problems. Wage claims ran even higher in the public than in the private sector, machinery wasn't properly maintained, raw materials were wasted. Far from their showing profits to fund additional nationalizations, the government had to subsidise them, and workers' demands went on increasing. It was like an infection —

when one group of workers made a demand, the next would make a bigger one. The situation was close to chaotic.

It was this which finally prompted us — the more radical parties — to produce our own version of participation. Instead of the official Production Committees we proposed much stronger 'Committees for the Defence of Production' (CDPs). Their members were directly elected by the workers, instead of consisting of union officials who weren't answerable to them. Union officials weren't excluded — but they had to be chosen in their own right. Secondly, the CDPs, through mass meetings, directly informed and consulted the workers on all aspects of production — budgeting, profits, planning options. Although one could exaggerate their contributions to these decisions, the workers put forward their own ideas — on how to improve machines, for instance, in ways which technicians had never noted. In exceptional cases, as I mentioned, this led to a complete overhaul of the whole basis of production. Also political questions were raised, like the role of unions in the process through which we were living, the results of wage demands etc.

The CDPs took root especially in plants where the revolutionary parties were strongest. Their intelligence commissions helped in this. When we learnt of some new right-wing tactic we'd publish it and inform the workers, through the CDPs and later the cordons. This meant that subversion not only failed, but united workers to defend production and the PU, through the CDPs.

The development of the CDPs varied from factory to factory. Typically, the original Production Committees turned gradually into CDPs, as events confirmed the need for these. There wasn't often a conflict between them. Nor was the legitimacy of the official unions questioned. The problem was that while the CUT was strong at regional and national levels, it was weaker at the base, which was now so crucial in the struggle — not because it lacked a following, but for want of local organization. The CDPs and later the cordons filled this gap. Their leaders never undervalued the CUT. Rather they hoped to persuade it to give the struggle a clear direction.

There were differences of opinion even within the radical left as to the extent to which the workers should control each factory's Administrative Council. We in MAPU felt that the MIR was obsessed with this, with 'workerism' (*obrerismo*). In the face of the mounting crisis, though, we overcame these differences. The first CDPs developed in the South, especially round Concepción, but by the time of the first bosses' strike, they'd spread to most industrial areas. We'd discussed coordination between them, but little had yet come of this, except in the strongest working-class areas like Maipú-Cerrillos and Vicuña Mackenna, in Santiago. The bosses' strike was final proof that this coordination was urgent. Immediately CDP delegates and union officials from different factories in the major industrial areas discussed joint action against the stoppage. Embryonic cordons already existed in vanguard areas. Now they spread to every big city.

This was done in the following way. Their immediate purpose was defined as the collective defence of production and of the PU government. Delegates to each cordon were requested from all the factories in its area, not just those of the public sector. Typically, most worker members of each firm's Adminstrative Council accepted. If they declined, though this was rare, the cordon's leaders advised the workers to elect a delegate for each section of the factory. The leadership met regularly and formed various commissions — transport, security, maintenance of production and so on. This working structure developed precisely in response to the needs of the moment. Again, there was suspicion that this was a form of parallelism, supplanting the government and unions — but the fact was that existing bodies just weren't adequate for the crisis. In our early attempts to solve the problems of distribution, we found that the state mechanisms, like the Ministry of Economic

Affairs, offered only the vaguest solutions. They couldn't maintain even minimal supplies of power or medical items, for instance. It was the workers, through the cordons, who decided to keep the factories producing when the bosses ordered them to stop. Cordon workers manned public transport and fought the lorry-owners' thugs to keep basic raw materials moving, organizing their own convoys between the ports and factories. They faced up to fascist squads and organized distribution centres in working-class residential areas. Together with the *campesinos* they set up markets, selling fuel, food and clothes; these markets were improvised, but immense. They were based on examples like those of the textile workers in Viña del Mar, who'd long since distributed their products direct to lower-income consumers.

While the CDPs had begun in the South, the first cordons were in Santiago, as it was there that the stoppage hit hardest. This shows how closely linked the cordons were to the solution of real problems. By the time the stoppage ended they existed at least on an improvised basis in virtually every major city. With the workers' understanding of what the bosses' strike had meant, they became the core of the revolutionary process — a means not only of defending but also of advancing the workers' gains. For instance, cordon leaders confronted the local authorities, including the right-wing ones, with specific demands: for workers' houses within reach of the factories, for example. We always encouraged cordon leaders to maintain immediate objectives like this, although the crucial issue was the class struggle, the question of power. We never forgot this, however far we may have been from carrying it through.

The missing factor at this point was a coherent political vanguard, united on a revolutionary strategy: the PU leadership had no answer to this stage of the confrontation. But in spite of this, and of disillusionment, these beginnings of popular power continued expanding right to the end.

The vanguard cordons developed into communal commands, which integrated the shantytown dwellers, *campesinos* and students with the factory-workers' organizations. This consolidated their previously improvised solidarity. For instance the communal command of Punta Florida, in Santiago, was recognized by the local authorities as a consultative body. The command was led by the cordon, but through it the shantytown dwellers in particular came to speak with a new voice. They disputed the local authorities' assumption that the main streets should be repaved when those of the shantytowns never had been; they demanded industrial estates to provide employment in the area. They backed the demands of the nearby *campesino* council for an end to delays over legal land expropriations, which the landowners and the courts were obstructing. Industrial cordons and the communal command took action to enable their *campesino* comrades to occupy the land and maintain its output.

None of this was straightforward. No process as complex as that of Chile, no revolutionary process, is pure. As a system goes into crisis and one form of society collapses, every social class is affected. Workers suffer, as well as the privileged, and like them they can be corrupted. For instance, while the bourgeoisie's sabotage instigated the black market, workers also contributed to it against the interests of their class. When Allende visited Sumar, a huge textile factory, he spoke openly of this — he told workers they could have covered the road from Santiago to Valparaiso with products which they had blackmarketed. It was their means of surviving the economic crisis. The important thing was that when the coup came, these Sumar workers fought the fascists empty handed. They held out for days against aerial bombardment. Yet even they had shown that the revolutionary process is full of human contradictions — that was how I saw it, how we always had to approach it. To do so in terms only of ideals as against objective conditions, is to fail to understand it. You have to remember that Chile's working class wasn't in power. We were barely beginning to establish forms of popular justice, for instance — the judicial system was still defending bourgeois interests. This is where the political vanguard is crucial — in creating the conditions to maintain the revolutionary process and overcome such contradictions. And this in my judgment is where the PU leadership failed in its final year.

The confrontation and the future: reflections

I believe it made two basic errors. The first was the incorporation of military men into the cabinet in moments of crisis — in the bosses' strike, and then again after the tank revolt (*tancazo*) of June 1973. This was a show of weakness. It seems that Allende, for want of a more effective answer, convinced himself that the military were neutral, not allies of the bourgeoisie. The second error was to curb the growth of working-class power in the hope of saving the situation with a Christian Democrat alliance.

Some comrades believe that the PU was merely reformist. This to my mind is a simplification. The problem was that having provoked pre-revolutionary conditions, it then stepped back, and this could only encourage the reaction. In the first bosses' strike, the bourgeoisie had been the loser. It attempted to bring down the government by economic means, but what happened? The workers stepped in and took everything over. They broke the boycott. The March elections of the following year dispelled the opposition's last hope of a democratic victory. Force became their only option, and therefore the one they were bound to adopt. This meant that the PU's struggle also had to be fought on these terms. The second stoppage, in July 1973, was thus quite different, a clear request for military intervention. At this point economic actions by either the bourgeoisie or the workers were not going to change the situation. Only the military apparatus of one class or the other could do this.

The bourgeoisie knew this. And so it won. It was not a new lesson.

The workers knew also, the vanguard at least. But what resources did they have against Hawker Hunters and machine-guns? Armed resistance would have been class suicide, in the absence of a political vanguard actively committed to it. Only this can split the army along class lines. The PU apparently hoped that this would happen spontaneously, and the workers paid dearly for this illusion. Their recognition of what was happening explains in part why the coup was so simple. Despite the cordons' determination, there was deepening disillusionment following the government's decision to rely on conciliation rather than popular organizations.

It was after the *tancazo* that this disillusionment became general. At this point the balance might still have been turned within the army, had the rebels and their supporters been crushed, as the workers were openly demanding. On the night of the *tancazo* Allende spoke to a massive crowd from the balcony of the Moneda Palace. People in the square were shouting up at him: 'arrest the plotters', and 'close the Congress'. Instead Allende presented the chiefs of the armed forces as the saviours of the day. Fights even broke out between supporters of his position and those demanding more radical measures. The latter were certainly a majority. But Allende maintained his position to the end, even confiding in Pinochet as the apparent leader of the constitutional wing of the army.

This speech from the Moneda was televised throughout the country. Everywhere the reaction was similar. Workers I talked to told me: 'We're through with politics. Comrade Allende would never betray us, but he has made a fatal mistake. Why should we fight when the battle's been lost for us?' In fact, like Allende, most of them did — even after the humiliation of the PU's allowing the military to ransack left-wing areas and torture activists before the coup. They fought on against the fascists and on 11 September died shouting for arms which never came.

This is not to say that the PU experiment was just a defeat. For one thing it showed that the working class is capable of challenging imperialism at its heart in Latin America. For another, any such experience is a lesson, if not a new one. Workers everywhere should remember that Chile was called 'the England of South America' for its alleged democratic traditions. If our experience reminds them of the nature of the bourgeois state and the seeds of fascism within it, Chile will not have been in vain.

For us the lessons are now very clear. There is no longer any midway between fascism and socialism. Chilean workers have no illusions about recreating the bourgeois state which international capitalism and national fascism have destroyed. Such a proposal would be to betray them. Also two left-wing strategies have now clearly failed in Latin America: the pluralist, reformist way adopted by the PU and equally the *foco* strategy based on the Cuban revolution. In recent years this has also failed to combine a revolutionary vanguard with a mass proletarian base — the essentials of any future way forward.

We're also realizing that with our commitment to this struggle our personal lives will have to be different. Our families, for instance, can't be what they were. I have to learn to know my children as people who may die in this struggle, like anyone committed to it. We're different people from the ones we were, yet still the same as other people whose solidarity we need — exeriencing fear, depression, contradictions, as well as hope. Things we can overcome only by continuing the struggle every hour.

3
Building the Industrial Cordons:
Maipú-Cerrillos

Speaker: PABLO, 25, activist of the Socialist Party who lived and worked in Maipú-Cerrillos, Santiago, a pioneer industrial cordon

Workers' participation in factories: origins of the industrial cordon

Maipú-Cerrillos is one of the biggest industrial zones in Santiago. Its population is over a quarter of a million and almost wholly working-class. The firms there range from affiliates of the multi-nationals to tiny workshops. Under the PU it was well known as one of the first and most advanced industrial cordons. I grew up and worked there, and was active in this process, as a trade unionist and member of the Socialist Party.

The cordon emerged in part from the question of workers' participation. The PU programme provided for this, but only on a limited basis, and mainly in nationalized enterprises. The government intervenor would set up an Administrative Council, with his own nominees in a majority over the workers' representatives. The government men were all technicians and this body made all the major decisions — over accounting and investment, production schedules, etc. The workers themselves had little influence.

Pretty soon a reaction set in, with comrades on the shop floor saying: 'It's time we made the important decisions. The PU is a workers' government. We're the ones who put them in power and argued for nationalization.' The problem was that the PU scheme was technocratic. It was far more concerned with production than with political questions. So the workers proposed a different scheme, in which they themselves would make the decisions.

The first instance of this was in the PERLAK detergent factory. I was there when it happened. The workers felt that nothing had changed with its nationalization. So they called an assembly and simply dismissed the Administrative Council, or rather voted themselves the right to have an elective majority on it. What they said was: 'Right, we're the ones to decide what policies this factory follows. From now on we'll deal with personnel. Full details of the balance sheet must be disclosed to all employees. We're also going to deal with production planning and distribution. We want to know who buys our products, because we want to work for everyone, not just for the wealthy.'

When this sort of workers' control was established, a new political awareness developed. The technical problems weren't neglected, but what came first were political aspects of the workers' participation. Activists like myself believed that as workers we should be our own bosses — that there must be a real change in the relationships of production. Factories should really belong to the workers — belong not in the bourgeois sense of being their private property, but in the revolutionary sense of belonging to a workers' State in which the workers made decisions. Only this would counter the bourgeois offensive which was developing from the outset.

In my experience this didn't prejudice production, as the Communist Party argued. In fact concerns under workers' control achieved the most success economically, as well as in a political sense. There was no conflict between the two. The workers worked and produced as before, the difference being that they now decided what they were going to produce, and also on its distribution. For instance, when meetings were held in work hours, the lost production was made up later with overtime or weekend work. The workers themselves enforced these rules, which meant a basic change of awareness.

You could see the same thing in the innovations which workers produced in these circumstances — in the local Nestlé's plant, for example, which also came under workers' control, following its nationalization. This also showed how technical factors weren't overridden by political debates, far from it. The Nestlé's products were expensive, way beyond most workers' pockets. The problem was how to socialize them while we were still in a market economy. We wouldn't gain anything by lowering prices and bankrupting the factory. So what did we do? We maintained the prices of traditional products with mainly middle-class consumers, and decided to launch a cheaper product for mass consumption, to be subsidized from our existing profits. It's here that the technical aspect comes in. The chief technician was fairly right-wing, but nevertheless this aroused his interest. He cooperated with the workers and left-wing dieticians to devise this low-cost product. The National Health Service had been trying to do the same thing for years and had failed. At Nestlé's they succeeded in two or three months — precisely because the workers felt, and even convinced the technicians, that it gave their work a social meaning. They also saw it as a test of workers' control and an answer to the propaganda against it. 'We'll show what we can do', was the way they put it. And that's how it came about, in no time, a cheaper and far more nutritious product. Workers' control produced any number of technical innovations like this, with a fundamental social importance.

Workers with these experiences supported the struggle in other factories for nationalization and workers' control. They knew that the process could survive only if it advanced. It was this which made them the vanguard of the Maipú-Cerrillos cordon.

Building the cordon

The industrial cordon really reflected the workers' growing recognition that only they could defend their interests — and that this must lead eventually to a confrontation with the bourgeois State. For this they needed an organization which was independent of it. It was precisely as the bourgeois counter-offensive developed that the cordons came into being, and were subsequently widened into the communal commands including local shantytowns and even nearby *campesinos*. Through the cordon the concrete details of the devolution of power began to be coordinated — food distribution, local transport, education and health measures and certain security provisions.

Each cordon was based on an important industrial area. It was in the first bosses' strike of October 1972 that they became widespread and their revolutionary role apparent. Of course in this sense they weren't part of the PU's electoral programme, and not all the PU parties backed them. The parties really committed to them were the Socialist Party and the MIR, the MIR especially in shantytown areas. Also later on the MAPU. Other parties disagreed at least with this interpretation of the role of the cordons. The Communist Party participated in them only once it realized how much power they had, and as we saw it, to neutralize them — which some of the Party's base opposed, producing a serious internal division. Its official line was that the cordons should simply support the PU, rather than becoming an alternative power (*poder alternativo*); whereas we argued that this depended on the PU's serving working-class interests. And this to our minds wasn't always the case.

This was very much the cordons' position, in that they confronted the bourgeois offensive while the PU tended to compromise with it. In these circumstances the workers felt that instead of simply depending on the parties, they should organize as a class vanguard. This is what the cordons reflected, and for this reason their main achievements were in cities where the working class was strongest — Santiago, Concepción, Valparaiso and Antofagasta. And eventually in smaller cities like Temuco and Constitución. The main ones in Santiago were Maipú-Cerrillos, Vicuña Mackenna, Estación Central, Barrancas and Santiago Centro. The first two depended almost entirely on leadership by factory workers. In Barrancas the shantytown dwellers also helped to show the way, as there weren't many factories there. Generally, though, cordons and commands were mainly led by factory workers. We discussed this a lot — the likelihood of their losing sight of the main objectives without such leaders. That this didn't happen, even in communal commands, was due I'm sure to their being acknowledged as the vanguard by all sectors.

My own experience was mainly in the Cerrillos cordon. This began to emerge in early 1972 — together with Vicuña Mackenna, it was about the first in the country. The starting point was a joint demand for nationalization by workers' leaders in several factories producing consumer durables — kitchen stoves and freezers etc. The idea was that cooperation would help them to deal with legal problems and to defend their industries against right-wing retaliation. From there they went on to coordinate their production schedules, particularly as the boycott by the private sector mounted, causing problems with inputs and so on. They realized in the most practical sense that these required joint solutions and a corresponding organization. From the beginning, what was to become the cordon developed in direct response to concrete needs, not to theoretical preconceptions divorced from what the workers wanted. And the first of these needs was the extension of nationalization.

This is the sort of thing that happened. The comrades would come to us — the workers and party members active in this process — and tell us: 'Look comrades, the boss in our firm is trying to cut back production and we're heading for a crisis.' They realized clearly that this wasn't just an incident, but — for the bosses and themselves — a crucial stage in the class struggle. So we'd tell them: 'Comrades, this is what you have to do. First, present all the evidence. We can then help with the legal aspects of your demand for intervention by the Ministry of Labour. And failing that, we'll mobilize.' It didn't always work out easily. Sometimes intervention was refused because the government was soft-pedalling the Christian Democrats, or even because the owners had influence — there were many reasons why the government was often reluctant. In these cases we had to bring pressure to bear, whatever the short-term repercussions.

Our strength always lay in taking joint action. The most important case of this kind was in July 1972. Five large firms, including Polyester Textiles, were occupied by their workers, who then demanded expropriation — of some because they were virtual monopolies, of others because they were cutting production. They'd already asked for intervention, but the government wouldn't give firm answers. So the workers said: 'Well, if they won't take over the factory, we will — we can't let things go on this way. If need be, we'll take this whole area over.'

This meant coordination on a scale no party activists had considered, but the workers themselves didn't hesitate — and where trade-union officials wouldn't support them, though this was rare, they overrode them. 'We've come to a deadlock — whatever happens, we're not stopping short. If it means a showdown with the police, we're ready for it.' So they mobilized, occupied the factories, hoisting the flag up on the roof, and demanded government intervention. The government again said no, that they were crazy. So the chips were down. An official from the Ministry of Labour came down to one of the factories and got into a confrontation with one of the leaders of the occupation — he was later murdered, during the coup. 'You can't do this to the Popular Unity', the official said. So the comrade replied: 'It's the bourgeoisie we're attacking, not the Popular Unity. If you take their side, that's your decision. Nationalize the factory, and we'll deal with the bourgeoisie together, which is a very different matter.' But this didn't work. The official just called him an ultra-leftist and a CIA agent. That got him mad. She, the official, had been a worker too, he said, but now she'd joined the bourgeoisie. That was too much for her — she gave him a smack in the face and left. We got no further answer, so the whole area was taken over. Barricades were put up across the two roads leading into Maipú-Cerrillos, cutting it off from Santiago. The *campesinos* chopped down trees and the workers added petrol drums. We told the Minister that we'd give up the area only when he came to sign intervention decrees in front of the workers. Soon afterwards he came and signed them.

This was the sort of concrete action from which the industrial cordon developed. The problem then arose — from about mid 1972 — of giving it some formal structure. At first the provisional leadership consisted mainly of local union officials, but few of them really involved their members in the issue of the cordon — they simply came as union officials and treated it as union business. Neither in principle nor practice were they representative of the workers with respect to the actual cordon. Then again, not all the factories in the area were involved. Also of course there were certain parties which told their activists not to take part. All these were serious obstacles.

Our answer was to try and relate the concrete tasks and political issues. We held discussions about how to democratize the cordon and through it avoid the differences within the left. Another goal was to include the shantytown dwellers and *campesinos*, but the question was, through what sort of structure? The most immediate problem was sustaining interest in the cordon. For instance, after participating in the campaigns for expropriation, many workers took no further part in activities at a cordon level. The groups of workers with such horizons, except at moments of obvious crisis, were

fairly few. Perhaps the main reason was the party activists'
vagueness as to the cordons' main objectives. In meetings they
tended to produce the same old ideological wranglings which
many of the workers detested. So they stopped coming. We'd
ask them about it: 'What happened, comrade? You came to
the meetings when the cordon was supporting your factory
occupation, but now we don't see you. What's the problem?'
'Well, we did go to later meetings — remember, we came to
three or four? But no one talked about anything concrete, it
was all fancy political stuff, and we prefer to be doing
something. Frankly we're not too interested in all that
discussion between the parties.'

The leadership did become more democratic, although it
still consisted mainly of union officials as delegates, until we
formed the communal command and all delegates became
elective. This was only right at the end, though, in June 1973.
Meanwhile the delegates' assembly elected a president and
vice-president, a comrade in charge of transport, another in
charge of food distribution, health and education etc. These
formed committees to deal with problems raised by the
delegates' assembly.

Support for the cordon depended on its achieving concrete
advances. It wasn't just a debating forum on soviets and the
bourgeois State. We tried to deal with tangible problems of
food supply and distribution, and cases of expropriation. On
the strength of this we did go forward from our originally
vague position to the point of even winning support outside
the factories, from shantytown dwellers and *campesinos*.
This meant that we were developing from the original
industrial cordon into the communal command.

*From cordon to communal command: factory workers
form the vanguard*

One central feature of this was the *campesinos*' participation.
Maipú-Cerrillos was somewhat unique for Santiago in
including agricultural units. In industrial zones like Vicuña

Mackenna there weren't any, though some in Concepción did have them. It was this which gave us a starting point for forming the communal command, with its wider basis.

In fact, the workers on these units weren't *campesinos* in the usual sense of people with close ties to the land — they were pure wage-workers. Also they lived within the community, not on the agricultural units, to which they simply went to work. This made them relatively aware. From the start they witnessed and supported the factory workers' struggles. They were unionized and had long since pressed successfully for the implementation of the original land reform, on properties over eighty hectares. Most of those in the area were smaller than this, though, but highly productive — market gardens of between forty and eighty hectares, selling their products in Santiago. One belonged to the son of Pedro Vuskovic, the Minister of Economics. Others were divided among different members of single families — a means of dodging expropriation under the agrarian reform law. The workers on these medium-sized, but equally valuable, units considered it wrong that they were exempted simply because they didn't cover eighty hectares. So the *campesino* council, with delegates from each farm unit, demanded immediate expropriation of holdings over forty hectares.

This was early in 1973. The *campesino* council had already supported the cordon in the occupations I described, and now they asked the cordon for its backing. We agreed, as their position seemed correct — they weren't asking for sub-division of the land, but for the more collective CERAs. The units over forty hectares were occupied immediately, with the help of workers from the cordon. Most were from the factories which had previously been expropriated with support from the *campesinos*. From this point on, in early 1973, there was virtually a permanent alliance between the two sectors — the basis of a communal command.

In these months events moved rapidly, as we were between the two bosses' strikes, which meant new tasks to undertake and a widening awareness of them. Our first step was a new leadership structure for the communal command, distinct from that of the cordon, which was now superseded. Delegates were now directly elected from each factory and farm unit, to form the assembly of the command. This then re-elected the president and the various committees on transport and so on. The assembly met regularly to discuss the committees' operations and had the right to revoke appointments. It also now included delegates from neighbourhood associations and JAPs (people's supply control committees). In this way the shantytowns and local consumers were directly represented. This structure was in operation by June 1973, the time of the second bosses' strike.

Another important novelty was the participation of women, which was almost unknown before the PU. They'd played an important part in the JAPs and now the health committee was organized mainly by women. They were also active in education and propaganda, though problems like security remained very much the domain of men — such changes came slowly.

Certainly the communal command was never a self-sufficient unit, as the coup was to show — though with the pace of change, a few more months would have made a difference. The cordon's original limitations were past history by this time, but the work of many of the committees was only beginning, especially security. As the bourgeois offensive mounted, we were dealing with problems on a day-to-day basis, without the time to find radical long-term solutions.

The key committees were those of supply and distribution, transport and health. Others also got well under way, especially the education committee. This set up libraries with books from the state publishing house, which was issuing low-cost editions of the political classics etc. This supplemented the new awareness which experience was creating. Even in those tense circumstances people read these books very widely. We also had talks and discussion groups at a popular level, with participation increasing steadily. In the health committee there were plans for creating multi-purpose clinics to serve the workers in the area and to be permanently staffed by doctors. Previously people had to go outside the area for medical treatment. The first clinic was built with voluntary labour by the health committee, and left-wing doctors began to work there — a gesture for which many of them were tortured and murdered after the coup.

Food distribution was a major problem when shopkeepers started joining they boycotts, so a people's market place was set up. This was quite a struggle. An unused area was chosen, belonging to the municipality, but as we had a right-wing mayor, he refused to let us use it. So together the *campesinos*, factory workers and neighbourhood associations occupied it, producing pamphlets explaining their action. The *campesinos* then came there and distributed their products through the JAPs and people's stores (*almacenes populares*). It wasn't just PU followers who bought their food there, but members of the petty bourgeoisie who couldn't afford black-market prices. This had an important impact. It showed that we could control distribution and also that the shortage was not the PU's fault but the private sector's. When the mayor tried to close the market, the whole community resisted. Right up to the coup this dispute went on but the market continued, thanks to the wide support we had.

This process produced a new generation of local activists. These were much more political than the older, trades-union leaders with their mainly economic concerns for better wages and living conditions. Most factories produced these new leaders, who seemed able to grasp the situation and pull the communal command together. One I knew well had little formal education, just a few years of primary school, and he wasn't really an activist when his factory was expropriated. Once it came under workers' control, though, he started taking a leading part and became a delegate to the assembly. All this was in a space of months. The same thing happened in countless factories and neighbourhoods, at a speed unique to a pre-revolutionary period.

The testing point of the command was the bosses' strike, the second one in July 1973, when most lorry-owners stopped work and private factories and stores closed down. This soon caused a shortage of raw materials, which threatened to halt production completely. So we pooled the trucks of all the factories in the command and coordinated our use of them. This was improvised, but we were strong enough to take over some municipal trucks and requisition private ones. Convoys then went to bring the food from the farm units. Most of the life of the area was run by the communal command at this stage. Factories also now sold direct to the consumers, and we set up special points for this — the main square of Maipú was one and another was the people's market. This went well beyond the role of the official peoples' stores, which lacked the versatility to deal with this situation. The trucks were simply loaded and driven to the distribution point, a ramp was set up, and the products were sold. The command's main distribution committee coordinated the local ones to deal with the details — each sector's requirements, the pricing and actual selling etc.

The assembly made the main decisions concerning the work of the committees. By now it was meeting almost daily, with over a hundred people present. Originally party activists had dominated its discussions, but this was changing rapidly. The great majority of those who came, including *campesinos* and women, were taking part and making suggestions almost without any hesitation. By now we had a genuinely integrated structure, and its impact was widening rapidly to the mass of the local population, as it proved able to solve their problems. I wouldn't say that even by this time the communal command was wholly established in people's minds or in place of previous institutions — after all, we're talking about a few months — but it was on its way towards this.

Meanwhile, as activists we were living with a day-to-day intensity which meant that most of us hardly slept. We had our committees in our places of work, party meetings, the assemblies — we hardly ever saw our families, sleeping away from home if at all. Yet at the same time we were all aware of the special nature of this moment. The parties all knew that a showdown was coming. But despite this knowledge, we had few resources for it. The ideological differences within the left were still too great to allow for coordinated action. It was only after the June *tancazo* that we started to mount a defensive plan for the full-scale coup which was clearly coming.

The coup: resistance and conclusions

All the parties involved in the command participated in this plan, but even so it was rudimentary. Time was short and the military were naturally suspicious of Maipú-Cerrillos. Four days before the coup, twenty truckloads of soldiers armed with machine-guns and mortars, moved into Cerrillos and set up camp. The arms searches grew more violent, but we imagined that their immediate objective was to demobilize the command — so our efforts went into providing for this, instead of preparing for the coup. When it came, we were virtually helpless. Maipú-Cerrillos was in the flight path of the jets bombing the Moneda. People were weeping, screaming at them, but what could they do?

Nevertheless there was widespread resistance, reflecting the structure of the command as the new vanguard of the area. Though many leading comrades had been captured during the previous night, it was the factories like PERLAK which put up the fiercest fight, some of them for four or five days. To understand what this represented, you must remember that we had only light firearms and home-made weapons against helicopters, which flew overhead and machine-gunned us from several sides. That was during the first two days. On the third they began using mortars and shells, and a number of factories were badly damaged. Their tactic was to strike violently, regardless of the casualties. The coup had to be rapid or mass resistance would have spread. The cordons and commands were especially feared, so they suffered the bloodiest repression. About three-quarters of my comrades in the Maipú-Cerrillos command were captured and many of them were later murdered. A few escaped, but very few, while some like myself went underground before the military caught us.

I don't want to give a false impression of the impact of the coup, though — in many factories political work is still going on, despite the repression. Comrades less openly compromised have stayed on and set up underground unions. Although the parties were so hard hit, there have already been several strikes in Maipú-Cerrillos. In these conditions they're dramatic proof of the organization and awareness achieved by the close of those three years.

What the left must do, not just in Chile, is to learn from these experiences, from their positive and negative aspects. To my mind the first lesson is the impossibility in practice of the peaceful way to socialism. If this is learnt, our defeat will not have been in vain. In countries like Chile, winning more or less votes is no longer the key to the achievement of socialism — it simply means more or less repression. The left has been idealistic about this. While mass consciousness is obviously central, the sheer technology of revolution is something we must consider more carefully. Without this the greater the mobilization, the more we are putting our heads in the noose. Our view of the bourgeoisie is outdated: it takes little account of its modern resources. Perhaps in Lenin's time there was some real ground to be gained within the bourgeois state apparatus. Today its counter-revolutionary techniques present a different situation. In Chile this meant the deaths of thousands of our comrades — we have to give this urgent thought, at the tactical and strategic levels. I suggest this less as a criticism of any particular left-wing party than as a problem for all of us. We must redefine the struggle for power from our own experience.

This is not to deny the continuing validity of basic Marxist-Leninist tenets. It is precisely in terms of these that we can redefine the problems. But perhaps the most important lesson which we experienced in Chile is the scope for widening people's awareness and giving it new, concrete forms. The cordons and commands were to my mind the PU's most significant feature. Through these, people were developing an answer to the power of the bourgeois State, an answer which could have meant victory if it had been more widely agreed on. This comes back to the negative aspects, but the price for these has been paid. The lesson is there for all to see. Recriminations offer nothing. Instead we should look at these positive aspects like the cordons and commands as a basis for new confidence and new ways of building socialism.

PART II
THE COUNTRYSIDE

Background

Every third Chilean works on the land. Traditionally this has been dominated by large landowners (*latifundistas*). Their properties were characterized by servile labour relations, low productivity and poor conservation. Most *campesinos* were either landless or smallholders (*minifundistas*), without enough land to support a family: this obliged them to work for the large estates. A well-known study in the 1960s found the following: 80 per cent of the land was concentrated into 7 per cent of all holdings, with many of the largest estates belonging to members of the same families; 70 per cent of all rural families earned less than $100 per year. The great majority suffered from malnutrition, illiteracy, inadequate housing and under-employment. Most *campesinos* knew little of the world beyond the local estate.

This situation obstructed economic growth. It restricted the market for manufactures and the countryside's capacity for meeting the cities' food requirements. It was also a source of mounting protest, backed by the Communist and Socialist parties, through the *campesino* confederation 'Ranquil', established in the 1930s. Hence in the sixties agrarian change became central to the bourgeois reforms which the Christian Democrats proposed, supported by the Alliance for Progress.

The policy of the Frei government was to foster rural capitalism by gradually expropriating the bigger, under-productive estates and encouraging commercial, medium-sized farms. Market pressures were tacitly expected to convert the smallholders into the rural proletariat which this policy also required. One large state agency (CORA, the Agrarian Reform Corporation) was responsible for the expropriations. Another (INDAP, the Agrarian Development Institute) dealt with socio-economic issues. All properties of over eighty 'basic' hectares (two hundred acres, measured in terms of productivity) would be expropriated. Owners would receive compensation and retain a medium-sized section. The rest would be transferred to the resident workers (*inquilinos*), initially as a cooperative (*asentamiento*). Later they could opt to divide it into private holdings. Meanwhile rural unions were officially recognized for the first time. These measures had different implications for the various categories of *campesinos*. They offered little to the great majority — the smallholders and temporary workers (*afuerinos*). Their political aim was to build a Christian Democratic base among the former resident workers, as the main beneficiaries of both land reform and unionization.

The Christian Democrats only partly fulfilled this programme. A hundred thousand families were due to receive expropriated land, but only twenty thousand did so. Unionization was limited mainly to regions controlled by the Christian Democrats' main *campesino* confederation, the *Triunfo Campesino*. Food production increased very little. By 1970 rural strikes were increasingly frequent and politically motivated. The *campesinos* also began to occupy properties whose expropriation was overdue. This sometimes ended in violent repression. As Pepe (ch. 5) describes it, all this convinced sectors of the left, particularly the MIR and MAPU, of the need to organize *campesinos* to press from below for greater changes.

The PU undertook to complete the land redistribution programme and to consider extending it to holdings of forty to eighty hectares. *Campesino* councils (*consejos*) would be established at the local and provincial levels for mass consultation over the programme. It was also eventually agreed that instead of cooperatives, the PU would introduce Agrarian Reform Centres (CERAs). These would be larger and better planned, combining a number of former properties. Also they would be more collective. All participants would have equal rights, including women, former smallholders and temporary workers. The bulk of profits would be reinvested; not divided.

The first proposal presented few problems. Expropriation of holdings over eighty hectares went even more rapidly than planned, due partly to the continuation of protest strikes and occupations. Within six months the PU redistributed more land than the Christian Democrats had in six years. By mid 1972 this part of the programme was completed. Remarkably, this was achieved without a fall in food production, despite sabotage by the departing landowners.

This raised the question of further developments in the PU's programme and also of its political purpose. Opinions within the PU differed on two central issues: whether to move rapidly toward socializing agriculture, and how much power to devolve to *campesino* organizations. As the right retrenched in the countryside, these issues became bound up with the problem of how the PU should confront it.

This debate was virtually the same as that on the industrial sector. The Communist Party, leading Socialists and the MOC were concerned above all with the battle for agricultural production, and the danger of driving the medium landowners into non-cooperation. A limited programme should be followed. The enemy should be clearly defined as the 'semi-feudal' big estate-holders, in order to retain the neutrality of the rural 'middle sectors'. This meant that the *campesino* councils should be subject to the central control of the PU leadership and the CUT, mainly through the rural unions. The socialization of agriculture was not crucial or feasible at this juncture, and should therefore be left till later.

However, sections of the Socialist Party, the MAPU and the Christian Left Party emphasized mass mobilization, the transfer of power to the councils, the collective organization of CERAs and the need to lower expropriation to a forty-hectare minimum, despite congressional opposition. In their view gradualism was more dangerous. It would alienate those *campesinos* demanding much more radical changes and fail to convince the less defined sectors, smallholders particularly, of anything but the PU's weakness. This would incline them to the right. The petty bourgeois tendency fostered by Christian Democrat reforms must be decisively confronted. The MIR was in broad agreement with this, and especially emphasized occupations by the poorest *campesinos*, such as the Mapuche Indians.

The outcome varied from province to province, depending on the local balance of power between the various PU parties within CORA and INDAP. As the speakers in this section indicate, CORA tended to be 'gradualist', whilst the notion of '*campesino* power' was more influential in INDAP. Both of them also convey the extent to which these positions were forged by events as well as theories — events which split the MOC from the MAPU, to which it originally belonged. For Enrique (MOC), who worked for CORA in the Central Valley, the *campesino* councils were secondary and the socialization of agriculture was at this stage a premature question. For Pepe, however, both have been central since his pre-1970 experiences with the Mapuche in southern Chile. *Campesino* power relates to the question of popular power generally, in the form of links between the councils and workers in the industrial cordons. The *campesinos* are vital to the resulting communal commands, and these are a crucial part of the answer to mobilization by the right — though others would argue that they aggravated and were unable to contain it.

There are, of course, some pragmatic grounds for each of

these two speakers' positions, deriving from their respective contexts. In the last analysis, however, they rest on the different strategies between which they were obliged to choose, for the achievement of socialism and the *campesinos'* role in this.

4
The Campesinos and Popular Unity: agrarian reform in the Central Valley

Speaker: ENRIQUE, 28, a lawyer and activist of the MOC, who worked in CORA, the Agrarian Reform Corporation, dealing with land expropriations in the Central Valley

Agrarian Reform: the PU develops a programme

During the PU, I worked for CORA in an area of the Central Valley — I'll refer to it as San Fernando. The Valley is Chile's most fertile region and traditionally one of large estates. Its market towns like San Fernando are completely controlled by the big landowners. In my three years there I experienced changes typical of those occurring in much of the Chilean countryside. Politically I belonged to a generation disillusioned by the Christian Democrats' failure. This led us to found the MAPU, and later the MOC, to which I belong.

I was involved in the transfer of land to the *campesinos*. This meant talking to them about the legal and technical details, as the PU laid great stress on maintaining democratic procedures. The central question, though, was how the land would eventually be worked — collectively, as private holdings, or on a mixed basis. Our usual recommendation was a mixed system for three to five years, then a final decision.

This process was naturally conditioned by what had

happened in the last few years. Under Frei the *campesinos* acquired the right to unionization. Though superficially progressive, this was shrewdly implemented. The bourgeoisie and its Christian Democrat politicans wanted an economistic, sectional *campesino* movement, not an independent, political one. So they created and controlled two *campesino* confederations, *Triunfo Campesino* and *Libertad*. This weakened the older, more radical Ranquil confederation led by the Socialist and Communist Parties.

Frei's reforms threw the left off balance, as it had pressed for them for years, only to see them introduced by a bourgeois government. At first this weakened the left's appeal to the *campesinos*, but not for long, as the Frei regime became less successful and more repressive. When expropriations fell behind schedule, the *campesinos* began occupying the big estates — but the government hit back by exempting these from expropriation. Also the programme was politically selective. The reforms were concentrated in areas controlled by the Christian Democrat confederations.

All this brought a rapid growth in *campesino* organization. The PU's rural vote in 1970 was bigger than we had expected, but still much less than the Christian Democrats'. Only after Allende's victory was there a dramatic reaction — an avalanche of land occupations, reflecting the last few years' frustration. In effect the *campesinos* were saying: 'One betrayal is enough, take note.' This was warranted — but for the PU the occupations were a problem. They were spontaneous and indiscriminate, occurring here, there and everywhere, on properties of quite different sizes. Even reformed *asentamientos* were occupied by landless workers. All this posed an obvious threat to the medium-sized rural bourgeoisie — the twenty-to-eighty-hectare-farmers whom the PU hoped to win over, or at least to neutralize. The occupations had to be checked, as the PU depended on legal procedures. One mustn't forget that in 1970 our victory was unexpected and fragile — its best defence, as Allende observed, was to stick to the rules. If only for this reason, we had to try to operate within a strictly legal framework.

On the whole we succeeded, by speeding up the expropriation of properties over eighty hectares. This brought home to the *campesinos* that the PU was their ally — and that some restraint was needed. The immediate pressure was relieved, except in rather special cases such as the Mapuche Indians, whose occupations were inspired by generations of collective memories of how the land had been taken from them. Apart from this things settled down. Even the industrial bourgeoisie was reasonably sympathetic to doing away with the big estates, as they obstructed capitalist growth.

The turning point came in the following year. The PU's programme — the elimination of 'large estates' (*latifundios*) — was ill-defined. Formally, it meant those over eighty hectares, but others envisaged going beyond this — a move which would threaten the modern agrarian bourgeoisie, not just the bigger, traditional holdings. This vagueness was typical of the PU. Probably it was the only means of achieving any consensus among the various PU parties. This was feasible at first, but once the first stage was implemented, positions had to be more precise. This brought the differences to the surface.

Moreover, as soon as the medium landowners came under pressure, the opposition coalesced. This class began to look for allies among the smaller landowners and also in the judiciary. This openly opposed the PU. It obstructed expropriations with rulings devoid of legal basis — for instance with 'measures for the defence of material interests' (*medidas prejudiciales precautorias*). These enabled rural magistrates to restrain even CORA from taking possession of properties due for expropriation.

In short, there was rapid polarization not only between the right and left, but also within the left itself on how to confront it.

The implementation of the programme: San Fernando

The debate on the left involved two quite different strategic conceptions of the PU's agrarian programme. One saw it as a holding operation, with the *campesinos* being won over by continuing land redistribution — though this would now be more effective and democratic than in the past. The other proposed more decisive moves to socialise agriculture, both in principle and as a means of providing for all the *campesinos*, including the poorest categories like migrant workers and smallholders. This divergence of views between a cautious and a radical approach was fundamental.

The PU's explicit programme was closer to the first position, but it still involved substantial changes. The Christian Democrat style of reform was blatantly paternalistic, as well as openly committed to expanding rural capitalism. Under Allende the *campesinos* began to participate in the programme. We were instructed to consult them on virtually every decision. This was unprecedented. Previously, for example, CORA even bought farm machinery for cooperatives without consultation. The *campesinos* just weren't involved in expropriations. No one asked their opinion about which properties should come first, and how best to set about it. The whole operation was bureaucratic, which is why it was ineffective.

Under the PU all this changed. The original schedule was to expropriate all holdings over eighty hectares within three years. But with pressure from the *campesinos* — to which the PU responded — this was later reduced to two years. Officials in each zone began by consulting the local *campesinos*. Meetings were called which often lasted for up to three days. These were attended by delegates of *campesino* organizations and even by non-unionized workers. Discussion was intensive. The *campesinos* would propose an expropriation programme for properties in the area. This was then discussed in the light of technical and political considerations: the soil conditions, for example, the sizes of the properties and the number of expropriations — as each region had an annual quota.

Political questions arose immediately. For instance, many *campesinos* worked in wretched conditions on medium-sized holdings, yet the PU was anxious not to encroach on these at this stage. This made little sense to the *campesinos* — surely, what mattered was their conditions? In answer we'd explain the alliances that we were trying to develop, and the legal constraints within which we were working. The atmosphere was deeply emotional — the *campesinos* were beginning to feel for the very first time that their world was in their own hands. When they realized that this time the land was really to be expropriated, they could hardly find ways to express their joy. This was even more marked at expropriation ceremonies, as these were attended by ministers and CORA officials who came right to San Fernando to formally transfer land titles. These usually took place in the local stadium. It would be packed with *campesinos* determined to witness a ceremony which signified such a change in their lives. They were unforgettable fiestas! You could sense that these people suddenly felt that society now recognized them as equals, as human beings who could make decisions. After the landlords' feudal sway, which had made them feel inferior to city-dwellers in every way, all this was a complete awakening. For us it was profoundly moving.

The land-reform unit we proposed was the CERA (agrarian reform centre). This was much more collective than the earlier cooperatives, which simply combined individual holdings. Also CERAs were run by all their participants, unlike the cooperatives, where hired workers had no rights in decision making. In CERAs there were no such workers, merely members of equal status, including women —though this found very little acceptance. One part of the CERA was designated as pasture, another for cultivation. The economic arrangements varied, but the basic pattern which we encouraged in San Fernando was as follows. Most of the land was worked collectively and the profits divided equally, apart from a margin of 15 per cent. This was put aside for reinvestment and social expenditures such as health and education.

The opposition story was that this was simply a state farm. The *campesinos* would ask us questions like: 'Is it true that on a CERA we'll be woken up at five o'clock by a man from the government blowing a bugle and ordering us all to work?' In fact the CERAs were midway between state farms and cooperatives. In any case they were provisional. Nevertheless the right's propaganda was sometimes success- ful, so that some *campesinos* did opt for the old, cooperative pattern. Some virtual state farms were established, known as production centres (*centros de producción*), but only in special circumstances. For instance when infrastructural investment in the property was high, or when it involved a strategic product. One in which I was involved produced certified rice seed for the whole San Fernando area — this made it especially important. Although this too involved *campesino* participation, it was run by a government official, with the last say in administrative matters. It belonged to the State, as did the profits, while the workers had a salary, a good one. But in fact these production centres were rare.

The CERAs naturally reflected the ambiguities of our programme, as an approach towards socialism within a still bourgeois society. In the main one I dealt with, two groups developed. One was more politically aware and all for collec- tive organization. The other was more individualistic. At first they agreed to make no distinctions with respect to rights and profits. This produced very good results. Productivity increased enormously. But soon their collective spirit weak- ened. One group started saying that they worked harder than the others, that they were more skilled, that it was unjust that they should own nothing privately and so on. For instance: 'I work harder than you, yet we both get the same, it's unfair.' Or: 'You were drunk on Sunday, you didn't come to work the next day, but I wasn't drunk, so I came to work — but we're still going to get the same, we have to divide things equally. That's not right to my way of thinking.'

Also with the better wages and purchasing power in the cities, demand went up and profits too, especially as the black market developed. This made them hanker after individualistic arrangements. This too was a product of our transitional situation — of our still having a market economy. So although both groups on this CERA remained PU supporters, the division between them grew deeper and deeper. Finally they divided the CERA. One part was still worked collectively and the other on a more private basis. To the end, these two groups remained in conflict. Similar divisions occurred elsewhere. My personal conclusion was that collectivization at this stage was utopian, in all but exceptional cases.

Campesino awareness: its limitations

What *campesinos* did develop was a new political awareness in the sense of an unshakable solidarity with the PU. For most of them 'socialism' meant simply Allende and the PU, but the class feeling in this was strong: it was they, the *campesinos*, together with the urban workers, who now had control of Chile's destiny. And they were determined that yesterday's bosses should never be allowed to regain it.

What grew was their sense of exploitation, rather than of socialism as a well-defined answer to it. For instance, I was once settling the details of expropriation with a landowner, when one of his *campesinos* appeared and overheard what we were discussing. It happened to be his reserve (*reserva*), the section of his property which a landowner was allowed to retain — always a contentious issue, as the landowner tried to get the best land and the *campesinos* to give him the worst. This itself showed how far they had come from their traditional subservience. On this occasion it really came out, as the *campesino* intervened: 'All this time you've been

starving us, and you still have the face to argue about
keeping the best land for yourself.' And so he went on,
berating him. But although they knew about exploitation,
their notion of socialism was vaguer — or rather, it was
much the same. 'Socialism means we'll be our own bosses,
that we workers will have our rights and that exploitation
will be ended.' This was how they'd talk about it.

Nevertheless, their determination put the PU under
pressure, and even forced us to alter decisions. With the
magistrates opposing reforms, the *campesinos* became
aware of the judiciary's class nature, and that of other
public bodies, including CORA. They sensed that this was
the root of the PU's limitations. This soon produced new
types of protest. Not only were occupations renewed when
magistrates delayed expropriations. Huge sympathy strikes
began as well, by *campesinos* throughout the area, over this
and over wages and working conditions on properties where
they were worst. This solidarity was quite new. For
campesinos to support others not personally known to them
was a real change, and it became increasingly common.

I'll give you an example of how this solidarity developed
— the origin of the CERA I mentioned, the one which
eventually divided. It also illustrates the exploitation which
lay behind it. A *campesino* came to my office and asked that
the property on which he worked should be considered for
expropriation. This was an almost daily event, so I told him
I'd look into it and give him an answer the following week.
But two days later he was back. We talked once more, and
this time he asked me to visit his home. It was as if he
couldn't rest until he knew that he'd convinced me. He was
an interesting character. He'd been illiterate, but taught
himself to read and write, and there was nothing he didn't
know about the agrarian reform.

Well, I accepted his invitation to visit the property. As we
went there, he told me various stories about it. One was a
vivid illustration of the world against which they were now
revolting. Ten years before the owner had forbidden the

campesinos to pass through his central grazing land, alleging that this encouraged stealing. One day a woman disobeyed, being pregnant and too tired to walk round. The owner set his dogs on her. They mauled her so badly that she died. I checked this story and it was true. Moreover, the owner had gone unpunished. Although a case was brought against him, he was only rebuked.

Shortly afterwards we did decide to expropriate this property. The owner — the same one who'd set the dogs on the woman — first had his lawyers try to bribe me. When this failed, he got the local Registrar of Properties to divide his land between himself and his two sons, into roughly forty-hectare units. Although this was illegal, it often worked, depending on the magistrates, as it could mean an appeal process lasting possibly for years. The *campesinos* heard about this and promptly occupied the property. They raised the flag, as they put it, expelling the owner and setting up the Chilean flag to demoralize potential attackers. And there they stayed. 'No one comes in except for our comrades — this property has been taken over.' The following day the magistrate ordered them to leave or face arrest. Their reply to this was to appeal to urban workers, through the CUT, and also the neighbouring *campesinos*. These helped them by setting up blockades and raising funds to support their struggle. In these circumstances the police stayed away, the government appointed an intervenor, and within weeks the property was expropriated.

Until it was settled, the *campesinos* continued the occupation. The owner meanwhile had mobilized the landowners' association. This brought the landowners face to face with the supporting urban workers — a situation which radically changed the *campesinos'* political outlook. Their submissiveness vanished. At the outset, their union belonged to the Christian Democrats' confederation, but after this they voted to leave it. As I mentioned, after forming a CERA, they had differences among themselves — but this never shook their common allegiance to the PU, which had resulted from this struggle.

These transformations weren't just political. The *campesinos'* whole outlook was changing. Their attitude to the cities, for instance. One *campesino* comrade told me how, whenever he went to the city, he felt awkward and out of place: he'd go there, get his business done and come back to the country as fast as he could. He saw it as a different world, where everyone looked down on him. For most *campesinos* the city was impenetrable and daunting, however desirable its attractions. After 1970 many of them told me how this was changing. The media helped to close the gap — with their improving standards of living, most families now had a radio, and most CERAs a communal television. Their new responsibilities and participation also helped. But what really made the difference was their new sense of identity with city workers. In the occupations like the one I described. Or in the PU demonstrations. Whenever these occurred in San Fernando, the visiting *campesinos* joined them, shoulder-to-shoulder with factory workers.

In effect their whole concept of space was changing, from one of total isolation. Traditionally, when a *campesino* was telling you where he was from, he'd rarely cite the nearest city, just the property and its owner. Often all he knew at first hand was this and the neighbouring estates. A trip to the city was an event. When they were round the fire at night, a common topic of conversation was what had been seen by someone who'd been to Santiago. For them to even begin to feel the social equals of city people was an advance.

Much remained to be learnt. Only the coup taught the real lessons, however much they'd already been mentioned — the class nature of the State, the extent to which their actions had challenged the basis of the system — all this they came to understand, but only at the very end. A few days after the coup, I remember, a group of *campesinos* told me: 'We never thought that our demands could end like this.'

This was after the event, though. Until then few

campesinos recognized the full depth of the issues. Their awareness was also limited by the uncertainties of the programme — as to whether it meant socialism, or just interim reforms. Once expropriation had removed the 'enemy', the old landowner, there was no clear way forward for them. I personally doubt if there could have been. What most of them still longed for at heart was their own patch of land whch they could work independently, and the security it offered. They'd sometimes say: 'We're against private property', but this wasn't borne out in practice. The landowners had encouraged this by allowing them small patches of land where they could grow things for themselves. This pattern was usually maintained in the reformed units, even the CERAs. They insisted on it, and fair enough, but the trouble was that it didn't stop there. They'd start with half an hectare per family, and CORA would agree to this, but within months this would start to creep up to a whole hectare, then two hectares. Neglect of the collective sector often led to heavy losses, while the *campesinos* individually might be making spectacular profits, usually through the black market.

A lot of resources were spent on ideological education, but in fact only concrete changes affected the *campesinos'* outlooks. Courses were combined with technical aid, on the assumption that socialism must be seen to give results. We emphasized that a collective system would raise their returns, not just their ideological standards.

Up to this point they could be sympathetic. The problems began with the question of how to divide the profits. This brings me back to the historical, transitional nature of that moment — one in which I just don't think that this problem could have been solved successfully. Expecting *campesinos* to share their profits was asking the impossible, while capitalism was still the rule. Their situation is quite different from that of a factory, which workers don't see as divisible into separate interests or set apart from the wider society — they have contacts in it and feel that they belong to a class, not just to a productive unit. Not so the *campesinos*. We'd spend weeks discussing collective work. We'd put it like this. 'How much will this land produce if one of you plants lettuces here, and another plants lentils over there? Compared to the yield if you all plant and work it together?' They were sometimes convinced, but it rarely lasted.

The nearest we got to socialist patterns was with the system of discipline which developed in some CERAs. Often it was more rigid than under the old landlord, as the *campesinos* now saw it as a question of common interest. In some cases drunkenness, even on Sunday — almost a *campesino* tradition — was regarded as possible grounds for expulsion, as it meant that the drinker might be unfit for work on Monday. One *campesino* told me that on his CERA this got to the point where they weren't allowed to celebrate or even drink in their own homes without asking the directorate's leave. Instead they'd arranged to have two big fiestas each year, during which there'd be no work and no restrictions. Systems like this were rare, though — *campesinos* remained suspicious of any authority, even their own, which tried to impose them.

The confrontation: the campesinos *in the last months of the PU*

For all their doubts on socialism, the *campesinos* reacted strongly to the right's increasing mobilization against the PU. Like every confrontation, it brought things out into the open. In the first bosses' strike, for instance, in October 1972, one good lady in San Fernando, an ex-landowner, drove round inciting the *campesinos* to strike. As they knew who she was, her actions couldn't have served us better — it produced the opposite of what she had expected.

The *campesinos* took a firm stand. 'It's obvious enough. The people to keep this country going are the ones who work. The idle rich won't stop it — if anyone does, it's going to be us. Otherwise it keeps working. If they want to stop it, we'll show them it doesn't depend on them, but on the workers and *campesinos*.' They meant this. They took over all fuel distribution in the countryside, for example, and transport to and from the city — on tractors, with goods piled high on the trailers. When this cut into their normal work, they added extra shifts at night. There'd never been so much petrol in the countryside as in that October, when the lorry-owners were trying to stop it and all the right was backing them. It enriched the *campesinos'* awareness of their own strength like nothing before it. You'd see them everywhere, with their wives and children, loading the trailers with essential goods for distribution. It was almost a holiday atmosphere, full of gaiety and banter, as well as new self-confidence. The second strike was similar — whatever its economic effects, it was another vital lesson for the people's political awareness.

This is looking ahead, though. After the first bosses' strike the fascist tendency of the right — the military, politicans, businessmen and the lorry-owners — was becoming more apparent. *Campesino* leaders got together to renew and extend the distribution measures which they'd developed in October. They now established rural distribution centres (*centros de abastecimiento rural*), warehouses at central points to which *campesinos* brought their products and sold them at official prices. They implemented these centres themselves, and they were popular and successful. Despite the right-wing propaganda and threats and sabotage against them, they kept food items available at official prices.

This new-found strength was centred on the *campesino* councils (*consejos*). These combined all the *campesino* organizations in the area, as well as non-organized *campesinos*: rural wage-labourers, sharecroppers, small-holders from the reformed sector and so on. Their role was seen in different ways by the different forces within the left. The PU leadership saw the councils as spokesmen for government policy — as a means of participation, yes, but within the dominant strategy of gradualism and non-provocation. Others within the PU regarded them as the seeds of what they described as popular power in the countryside — a necessary antidote to a government compromised, in their view, by working within a bourgeois context. They argued that the PU should devolve a proportion of its powers to these councils created by the base. The reply was that the highest expression of popular power was the PU itself, as a workers' government, whatever the limitations imposed on it by the bourgeois State. Independent initiatives by 'popular power' organizations — or, in effect, the parties behind them — were a dangerous parallelism. At worst a betrayal of the PU.

This was one of the issues that split the MAPU and led to the MOC, which I myself joined. Broadly speaking, I was convinced by the PU leadership's position, in terms of my own experience. In San Fernando the issue was something of a stalemate. The *campesino* council just didn't function as an organ of 'popular power' in the sense of taking independent, effective decisions. Partly because it was given no such power, but also because of its composition. In the countryside generally, few *campesinos* are wage-earners. There was thus no means for this one truly revolutionary sector to be the vanguard of the council. It was dominated by smallholders, including the cooperative sector — a group with decreasing sympathy for a revolutionary process. To my mind devolution to it could therefore even have strengthened the right. In any case our local council didn't urge it.

Nevertheless the *campesinos* were being increasingly radicalized. This was obvious in the mid-term congressional elections in March 1973. As elsewhere these usually go against the government parties, but this time the whole working class, *campesinos* included, was on the offensive — not against the PU, but against those sabotaging its efforts. There was inflation, food shortages — the ideal preconditions for a government defeat. Yet by now people understood that these were not the government's fault, but that of the right and the bourgeoisie. With three years' experience the *campesinos* could now see through right-wing propaganda. For instance they'd seen that all the tales about state farms were idiotic. This sort of thing had undermined the right's traditional credibility. If anything, their propaganda now had a negative effect. The *campesinos* noted carefully the opposition's stated aim of winning the two-thirds control of Congress needed to impeach Allende. 'They want to throw comrade Allende out, we won't let them do it.' This simple argument was a real mobilizer. 'They want to throw Allende out because of the expropriations. They won't, because we're going to defend him.'

Traditionally the *campesinos* had always voted as their landlord ordered. 'So-and-so's the one,' he'd say. The *campesino* simply had no other source of information, like activists or union leaders — the landlord forbade them to enter his property. All this had been changing since 1970, mainly in the PU's favour — the Christian Democrats' hold declined as the *campesinos* recognized their increasingly right-wing position, in alliance with the National Party. This even came to the point of their driving out *campesino* spokesmen for the Christian Democrats, and telling them never to come back. They rightly saw them as allies of their former landlords, and this was something they couldn't forgive them. In one case a right-wing senator was visiting a former landlord, who summoned the local *campesinos* to hear him. But as soon as he started to speak — and this was unimaginable a few years back — the *campesinos* shouted him down, so that finally he had to leave. With his tail between his legs, as the *campesinos* put it. This incident made quite an impact — rumours travel fast in the countryside, and this candidate ended up with hardly a single vote from the area.

The PU's rural vote was a marked improvement on 1970,

despite the problems we were facing. But this, if anything, reinforced the determination of the right. Its boycott of agricultural production had been highly organized from the outset. While the reforms were criticized for causing shortages, the real reasons for them were quite different. As soon as Allende came to power, the ranchers started removing their cattle over the border to Argentina: stocks were soon halved. When landlords knew that they were due for expropriation, they immediately stopped planting and removed the machinery etc. The *campesinos'* answer was resolute. Often, to maintain production, they'd go and plant with their bare hands. Otherwise production for the whole season would be lost. Up to 1972 this sabotage by landlords did produce very serious problems, but subsequently the balance was turning. Production schedules went up steeply in San Fernando. Take wheat, for example. By August 1973 we had already exceeded output for the whole of the previous year, and we still had a second crop to come. All this fell into the hands of the junta.

What we underestimated was the right's adaptability. The National Agricultural Society, once the preserve of the biggest landowners, became an increasingly militant organ of all the agricultural employers. It mobilized increasingly widely, especially at local levels. In San Fernando, immediately after the 1973 elections, small landowners' associations began to develop. These were directed by the former bigger owners, some of whom still had their reserve. The other members had anything down to a few hectares. It was on this basis that fascism began to develop in the countryside, inspired by the big bourgeoisie, but using the fears which they aroused among smaller owners.

At first this movement was less violent than in many other areas. But as agitation, it was efficient. Once when I was using the phone at a property being expropriated, I saw on the table the owner's instructions for mobilizing the smaller owners for actions against the *campesinos* — a system of communications and meeting points for their cars and tractors. As time went on they turned their attention to the cooperatives, even. Inflation, the profits of the black market, the shortage of inputs, all the factors resulting from producers' boycotts, contributed to this alliance. But we could do very little about it. Its basic strength lay outside the country, in the cities and at the national — and international — political level.

The terror and the coup in San Fernando

The March elections convinced the right that their chances of retaining power by legal means were now past history. Their first response was the *tancazo*, the armoured regiment's rebellion. Like the stoppage earlier, this produced some positive results for the left. As always it was events, not theories, which raised popular awareness. The *campesinos* stood unhesitatingly by the PU. As soon as we heard of the rebellion all rural properties were occupied, in accordance with the CUT's instructions. These provided for a general strike and occupation of factories and land in the event of a military coup. It was one mass occupation. The *campesinos* were ready to defend Allende with their lives. The whole thing was over by midday, but from that moment on *campesino* leaders were increasingly aware of the crisis. Whenever Allende or other PU leaders mentioned the need to maintain production, the response was immediate. They starting working incredible hours including night shifts. They held back on demands for price increases and stepped up direct distribution, independent of private retailers.

This was their mood when the final stoppage of the lorry-owners, retailers and professionals began in July and August. The right responded with the terror campaign which turned out as a prelude to the coup. When the *campesinos* went out with their tractors, they were stoned by organized fascist bands. By now the military and police were just standing by and watching all this, and most *campesinos*

PERLAK. Managed and controlled by the workers. Workers Management Committee of
PERLAK Factory, Maipú-Cerrillos (ch 3)

OUT! Gonzalo Lopes. Factory Occupation and Demands for Nationalisation

Against the Bosses' Stoppage—Workers to the Offensive!
Demonstration, October 1972, first bosses' strike'

The people's president. Allende talks to copper miners

We'll stand by our pledge to the Chilean people.
Trades union sections of PU demonstration, Santiago

Public Works Department, Workers Control! Demonstration, Santiago

Workers' Power! Wall painting

Commandeered! Left wing militias guard public transport during the 1973 stoppage

People's Power! Left wing demonstration, Santiago, 1973

Down with the Government! Christian Democrat banners mingle with those of the Fascist Fatherland and Freedom Party, right wing demonstration, Santiago 1973

The Coup. Santiago 11 September 1973

Campesino demonstration

This property has been taken over by the campesino council.
Land occupation of agricultural holding (Maipú)

Shantytown, Santiago

Revolutionary Left Movement—Campamento New Havana The New Havana (ch 6)
detachment in a PU demonstration

were unarmed. They kept trying to get produce through to the towns, but soon they were having to turn back daily.

In San Fernando the terror mounted. Enormous explosions shook the town almost every night. A few minutes later the local right-wing radio station would announce the result. 'The bomb that just went off was in the house of so-and-so, municipal councillor, member of such-and-such a party' — invariably one of the PU parties. Five minutes later another explosion, and a similar radio announcement. It was clearly a run-up to the coup, a systematic intimidation of PU supporters. It created an atmosphere of total terror. No one slept. PU supporters patrolled the streets but to little avail. My house was bombed twice. The second time the louts who'd thrown the bomb were detained, but soon afterwards they released them. They didn't even take their names. We put the children to sleep elsewhere and sealed all the windows and doors — those last few weeks were a time of sheer terror. The fascists' plan was working perfectly. When the coup finally came, most people were so intimidated that mass resistance was out of the question, despite the CUT's long-standing instructions.

By mid-morning on 11 September, the military had taken over all communications in the area. There was no contact with the government, and the radio began blaring the military's fascist propaganda. They threatened to shoot every single resistor, armed or unarmed. To my knowledge there was only one case of armed resistance in the area, but it was a massacre — *campesinos* resisting with .22s against machine guns. No one survived. Many people did stay in their places of work, offering the passive resistance agreed on. The military went round systematically ordering everyone to leave, then executed those who refused. They included many *campesinos* whom I had come to know in the area.

I was arrested two days later. My interrogation was a farce, because the idiots questioning me hardly understood their own questions. They beat me about a lot, demanding a confession that I was a Marxist, and asking me where 'the

weapons' were. They used all the standard tricks. Once two
of them were interrogating me with another comrade, for
instance, and one took him out and I heard a shot, and the
other who'd stayed with me said: 'He's dead, you'd better
talk fast.' And so it went on. I was there for ten days before I
got out, by means which I can't now disclose. There were
nearly three hundred of us in a room about ten by twenty
metres. We were literally piled on top of one another. I got
off lightly. Other comrades were tortured daily. Some had
their arms broken, others their teeth. Some disappeared.
Several went out of their minds, mainly those who were
submitted to simulated executions. They were blindfolded,
put up against the wall and given the last sacraments, then
blank rounds were shot. Some of them, even after it was
over, were convinced that they were dead. Imagining
everything was some. dream. Most of us were tortured with
electric shocks. One comrade was stripped and hung by his
feet from the ceiling and strangled so violently that his
throat was reduced to a pulp. It was like a nightmare
underworld, Dantesque. In the evening they'd let us out for
a while, then we'd go back in to try to sleep, piled on top of
one another. To wear us down, they kept loudspeakers
blaring all night with military marches and propaganda.

One thing we noticed was that few key activists were
there. This kept people's spirits up — it suggested that the
party structure was intact. Most of the prisoners were from
the base — *campesinos* and workers. The sense of solidarity
was as deep, perhaps deeper than before. Sometimes, in the
evenings, when people's spirits often went down, some of the
comrades would put on charades, to see us through. The
little food we got was shared. When I first arrived, at two in
the morning, two or three *campesinos* offered to share their
ponchos with me, as the guards hadn't given us blankets.

Even after I got out it was hard to come by information.
But I did find out that the military had summoned surviving
campesino leaders and told them that there would be no
changes: that the junta wasn't against them and the

expropriations would stand. Soon afterwards, though, properties were handed back to their former owners. In spite of the terror, the news spread like wildfire. Some of the better-off *campesinos* were seduced by the promise of firm land titles, but very soon they were having to sell them, and realizing that they were returning to the old system of land concentration. Meantime those who did speak out began disappearing. The repression was getting more systematic.

But so too was the determination of most *campesinos*, even then. One shouldn't underestimate the military, at least their powers of repression. But at the same time it would be a mistake to forget the half a century behind the workers' movement in Chile, as well as what happened in those three years. Whatever they do, they can't be repressed.

5
The Campesinos and Popular Power: building the revolutionary alliance

Speaker: PEPE, 31, MAPU activist who worked for INDAP, the Agrarian Development Institute, in southern Chile and later in the central provinces of Aconcagua and Valparaiso

Experiences in southern Chile: the Christian Democrat reforms and the case for a revolutionary programme

In 1965 I started working as an agronomist in southern Chile, in the province of Cautin, for INDAP — the agency dealing with technical aspects of the agrarian reforms of Frei. The local *campesinos* were some of the poorest in the country. Many are Mapuches, indigenous Indians, the only ones who resisted the Spaniards right into the nineteenth century. Once they were finally defeated, they were confined to reservations (*reducciones*). These were too small to support the number of people on them, and usually comprised the worst land. The best of it went to the big landowners, and these were forever cheating the Indians out of what little land they still had. Typically they'd lend them money, then demand their land as repayment. Or they'd get them drunk and persuade them to sell it. Instead of protecting Mapuche interests, the Institute of Indian Affairs (*Instituto de Asuntos Indígenas*) was controlled by the right and legalized these transfers of land, which were known as

'running the fences forward' (*corridas de cerco*). Often they
were just that — boundary markers would be moved, and
their new positions legally sanctioned.

In this way the Mapuches were pushed to the margins of
Chilean society. Better-off families had maybe one hectare,
some even less than a quarter of a hectare. This they
supplemented by working on the big estates for miserable
wages, the lowest in Chile. They were always on the hunger
line and hardly felt themselves to be Chilean. Many of them
detested 'Spaniards', as they still called non-Mapuches. The
feeling was mutual. Other Chileans regarded them as
drunkards and thieves, and they sometimes did have to steal
to avoid starvation. They had no effective rights as workers.
Their employment was temporary, and a working day was
from dawn till dusk, often fourteen hours. Minimum wage
laws were ignored and their housing and health conditions
were terrible. They had no bargaining power. If the farms
had been smaller and closer together, they might have been
able to organize, but conditions made this difficult — the
distances, working hours, the hunger.

The Christian Democrat reforms made little difference in
Cautin. Many properties were just under the eighty-hectare
limit, and the owners of the bigger ones divided them among
their children, to avoid expropriation. Overall the reforms
were token, often opportunist. For instance, take the law for
the unionization of rural workers — it actually weakened
them. Not only was it difficult for them even to form a
branch — which had to have a hundred members — but the
Christian Democrats founded two confederations, so that
those who were unionized could never put their weight
together. In a typical zone you'd find one branch belonging
to *Triunfo Campesino*, another to *Libertad* — both
Christian Democrat-controlled — and a third belonging to
the left's Ranquil. Probably there'd also be a smallholders'
association (*Associación de Pequeños Agricultores*), say four
in all. They couldn't possibly face up to the big landowners'
association, the National Agricultural Society (*Sociedad*

Nacional de Agricultura), controlled by the right-wing National Party.

Even INDAP's technical assistance was paternalistic and ineffective. It consisted mainly of credits, which smallholders often couldn't pay back — it seemed little more than a buying-off process, to keep them from absolute hunger and protest. This made many of us younger members of INDAP deeply frustrated. We'd gone into this field with some ideals, though many of us, including myself, had no political commitments. These experiences produced them. Many of us joined the MAPU, looking to its partly urban base to help build the worker-*campesino* alliance. Only this, we felt, would provide reforms to genuinely affect the Mapuches and others like them.

I was responsible for eighteen *campesino* committees, or provisional union branches, some consisting of Mapuches, others outside the Mapuche areas. Each had sixty to eighty members, the purpose being to give them technical help and credit. It was difficult work. Their every involvement with Chilean society had meant increased exploitation: first we had to convince them that we weren't there to steal their land, as experience led them to expect. Their first instinct was to avoid us, or ask us to leave the reservations. At first this really upset me.

I later learnt to go slowly. I'd go round the reservation with them, where they were going, not where I wanted to, or I'd work with them, at their manual work, without at first trying to make any changes. Eventually they'd take me to their homes. Sometimes I'd stay there, and they'd get to know and trust me. Only then I'd suggest a meeting of all the members of the reservation, or of all the local *campesinos*. I'd put it to them that our technical assistance wasn't enough, that they'd have to struggle for more basic changes. For the restoration of their land. For better terms of employment. For a local school — many Mapuche children had no means of getting to one. For the prompt reform of the big estates, so that future changes could be based on local planning, not just piecemeal.

The *campesinos* already knew that these were the important issues, but now they saw that some of us were recognizing them — and this offered new possibilities. They began to form *campesino* councils of all the committees and union branches in an area, to develop joint programmes — the expropriation of particular estates, the building of a road and so on. The councils launched land occupations to force expropriations through before the landowners sub-divided. This already foreshadowed the PU situation, when it was equally true that real changes depended on pressure from below, from *campesino* councils etc. Of course, these councils and their proposals were beyond INDAP's official programme, and much more revolutionary. Meanwhile INDAP was recruiting new staff through the usual Christian Democrat channels; but most of these were young and rapidly came to share our position, because it arose from results, not theory. Like I said, I and many others still had no party affiliation, though I felt myself to belong to the left. When the councils were formed and the land occupations began, we were immediately accused of being 'Communists and subversives'. All sorts of pressures were put on us, but they only brought us closer together and forced us to define our position.

Of course this was happening elsewhere in Chile — I'm talking now of 1968-9, the close of the Christian Democrat period. One national result was the formation of the MAPU, which most of the younger staff of INDAP immediately joined in Cautin. This provoked a sharp reaction from our Christian Democrat superiors. They harassed us in every way, transferring us from one region to another, to try and force our resignations. So INDAP struck, or rather most of its junior staff did. We occupied its offices throughout Chile. In Cautin we even held a joint meeting of all the councils in the province. This was in Lautaro, in May 1970. The *campesinos* supported us fully, and helped us to occupy the offices. Of course they were

active in other provinces, but nowhere else were they so
organized. Later there was an inquiry, and I was charged
with being responsible.

The next day they transferred me to San Felipe, in
Aconcagua, a thousand kilometres from Lautaro, way up in
the Central Valley. They gave me four days to get there.
Other comrades were also transferred. We consulted with
the *campesinos* — many of their leaders were now members
of MAPU. They offered to fight to keep us there, by
reoccupying the INDAP offices. The government could
hardly overreact with the elections in the air. But we
decided that mass pressures should all be turned towards the
campaign — the important thing was that the *campesinos*
had discovered their strength. Individuals were less
important, and the same work had to be done elsewhere.

So in May 1970 I arrived in Aconcagua. I brought with
me the lesson I'd learned in Cautín — that the only means of
changing the *campesinos'* lives was a revolutionary programme, and that this meant strength and pressure from
below, through the *campesinos'* own organizations.

Aconcagua: the campesinos *and the elections*

Aconcagua's very different. It's a wealthy agricultural zone
of medium as well as poor smallholders, alongside the usual
big estates. It was a Christian Democrat stronghold. Of the
thirty-three functionaries in INDAP, all but one were
Christian Democrats. They also controlled the rural unions,
apart from a couple belonging to Ranquil, the left-wing
confederation. On most estates there was no union or
provisional workers' committee — the old order was
unchanged and there was no way of penetrating them. The
smallholders also had some associations, but among these,
too, the left was weak. The MAPU was virtually non-
existent.

Luckily, though, my closest colleague was also disillusioned with the Christian Democrat reforms. We became

close friends and fairly soon he joined the MAPU. I was
dealing with the technical and he with the social
organization. By the time of the election campaign we'd
already put the MAPU's position across, and some
campesino leaders were with us.

Though this was a wealthy area, its social conditions were
as bad as Cautín's. The agrarian reform had made little
impact. Wages were wretched. The *campesinos'* houses, as
everywhere in the Central Valley, were made of adobe —
one-room houses, sometimes divided by a curtain, with a
lean-to kitchen. In heavy rain they often collapsed.

Our work began in Catemu, a smallholders' zone still
dominated by large estates. The smallholders wanted to
form a committee to channel technical assistance. We went
there from INDAP to supervise elections to it. In the
discussions three smallholders insisted that real changes in
the area depended first and foremost on expropriating the
estates. As the reforms were going so slowly, they concluded
that this would depend on themselves and not on public
functionaries. These three and two other young people were
elected as officers of the committee. They proved vital to all
our work in the area.

Very soon they were members of the MAPU, and helping
us in the campaign for Allende. They set out to convince the
other smallholders and workers on the neighbouring estates
that there had to be effective changes. This work was
clandestine — if it had been open, we'd have been banned
from the estates. These three comrades would contact
friends on an estate, and we'd meet in one of their houses at
night. We went on foot, as a vehicle would have attracted
attention. Three or four *campesinos* would be waiting and
often we'd talk through the night. We'd discuss how to press
for basic changes if the PU were elected, and how the
Christian Democrats had obstructed them by dividing the
unions. The Catemu comrades did most of the talking.
They'd put it quite simply to the others: how could they
expect changes from Christian Democrat politicians, when

these were often landlords or their relatives, or lawyers?

Without these three we'd have got nowhere. They made all the contacts. As public functionaries we weren't allowed to be politically active, though of course the Christian Democrats were — but they were in power. But the situation was also difficult for the three comrades — many a *campesino* had been bought with Christian Democrat favours. They had to tread as carefully as we did. As the weeks went by, we developed PU cells on most estates. We never held public meetings — these cells would continue on their own, each person talking to those he knew well.

The PU's base grew rapidly from these beginnings in Catemu. It also spread to the tiny mines in the sierra, with only a few workers each. Many of them came from estates, so this was another good source of contacts. They also helped us penetrate the *asentamientos*. Often these were harder ground than even the unreformed estates. The Christian Democrats, after all, had made them miniature landowners. An *asentamiento* of a hundred people might have only two or three left sympathizers. These comrades from the mines had courage, as the Christian Democrats had organized a real Mafia in these strongholds. If they discovered left activists on an *asentamiento*, they'd give them a hiding. *Campesinos* don't mess about in these matters — no talk, just blows. Our advantage was the sharp decline of the Christian Democrats nationally. Even Christian Democrat *campesinos* preferred Allende to the National Party's Alessandri.

Nevertheless, the PU made few gains in Aconcagua. This was true of most of the countryside, with the Christian Democrats' hold on it. These comrades' help did win new votes though. More important, we laid the basis for what followed, with the PU in power.

Launching and defining the struggle: unionization and class alliance

Like any government the PU felt that only its supporters would implement its programme fully. Within a short while I was head of INDAP in Aconcagua. Although most of its staff were still Christian Democrats, others did come over to us. Of course this made it much easier to launch the PU's measures.

The first was one on which all sectors of the left agreed; to increase unionization among the workers on estates, including those below eighty hectares which were exempt from expropriation. The MAPU's later position went beyond this; to combine all types of rural workers into *campesino* councils, and over this there was disagreement, particularly with the Communist Party. However, we were all agreed on this prior need for unionization and for completing the expropriation of properties over eighty hectares. In the MAPU's view this would have to be backed with land occupations if necessary — if the landowners opposed it, or if CORA hesitated, as the Christian Democrats still controlled it. So during this first year our target was the large estate.

The Christian Democrats' recognition of rural unions was only weakly implemented. In Aconcagua in 1970, less than a third of rural workers were unionized. This was INDAP's first priority. The Christian Democrat Confederation, *Triunfo Campesino*, was strongest in the area and so we urged its leaders to help us. We'd call meetings in non-unionized areas to persuade the *campesinos* to form one. Once a hundred wanted to join, elections were held for the positions in the union, which was then legally recognized.

We spent days with them, mapping out a programme. INDAP's resources were put at their disposal, and we went round the farms and estates together. The first step was to form a workers' committee on each unit. On the big estates this committee would then demand expropriation; on smaller ones it would organize to improve the wages and working conditions.

The landowners were all against unionization; they had no legal right to obstruct it but they invariably did so. Their powers of intimidation were enormous. Whatever the law, the only authority known to the average *campesino* was the landlord (*patrón*). So we still had to count on discreet persuasion. The *campesinos'* first thought was usually the landlord's reaction to unionization. In most cases it was quite clear; any worker who joined a union was out — out of a job, out of his house, and off his plot of land on the farm, where he'd probably lived all his life, hardly knowing even the nearest town.

I remember a typical incident in this campaign for unionization. I arrived at a farm of some sixty hectares with representatives from the *Triunfo Campesino*. The owner met us at the gate. The foreman and some workers were with him. They were armed and had two mastiffs on a leash. The neighbouring farmer must have sent word that we were coming. The owner didn't even open the gate. 'I know who you are. You're the agitators who are driving the owners off their land. Get out, or I'll set the dogs on you.' So I showed him my INDAP papers and explained that we'd come about unionization, an official government measure. This had nothing to do with expropriation, we explained. So he turned to the workers. 'Do you need a union? Do you have any problems?' 'No, sir.' 'Tell the Communists you don't need a union.' 'We don't need a union.' So I explained that he had no right to forbid us to enter. He could attend the meeting but if he went on threatening us, he was putting himself above the law and I couldn't answer for the consequences. Reluctantly he let us in, and heard us talk to the dozen or so workers. As usual we explained to them what unionization was about — their rights on wages, housing, working conditions etc. We told them a branch was being formed at a meeting that night, outside the farm. We asked them if they had any questions or problems which they wanted discussed, but they said no — the landlord was still there. We made it clear that if he prevented them from attending, the union could take legal action.

About half of them came, the young people mostly. I talked to them, but they said very little. They were nervous and kept to themselves. Then, as the hall filled up, they began to mix with the others and talk. In the end there were over a hundred *campesinos*, so we were able to form the union, including them as members. Afterwards we talked again, about the committee they'd have to form, to negotiate with their landlord. Their manner had changed. Seeing a hundred of their comrades from other farms, some known to them, had given them confidence already. They told me what the landlord had always said about unionization — if they meddled in it, they'd be out, and he'd ensure that they'd never get work on any other farm in the province. And now they admitted that they'd always had problems — wages way below the minimum, bad housing, long hours, threats from the foremen. They went back and formed the committee, eventually all the workers joined, and conditions improved dramatically.

Results like these were our best propaganda. Within two years 80 per cent of rural workers in Aconcagua were unionized, but farm by farm, struggle by struggle. Right to the end we had little impact on the more isolated farms, where the workers remained in the landlord's grip. For the others, though, it was broken. He was now obliged to negotiate with union officials, in front of the workers and with witnesses to every agreement. As the unions got stronger, the owners had to agree to the legal norms — or they faced a strike with support from other union members, or even an occupation of the farm. The servility of the past almost vanished.

Typically, the owners who resisted weren't the wealthiest — they were often those with some sixty hectares, and perhaps a dozen workers. Although they weren't due for expropriation, the bigger landowners dominated them. Their National Agricultural Society convinced these medium-sized owners that they would be expropriated and encouraged them to boycott production. And they believed them, although they were actually benefiting from the increased demand for food and better technical assistance. These fears were self-fulfilling. We in the MAPU were convinced that this would always be their position, that as the new rural bourgeoisie, they would boycott the PU, come what may. So we did feel that this sector would have to be expropriated for the reforms to be successful.

This raises the whole question of strategies for the rural sector among the PU parties. As I said, all of them were agreed on the need for further unionization — as were some Christian Democrats. But this was only the beginning. It raised the question of unionization for what end, apart from improving working conditions? We insisted that unionization should be the keystone of socialist goals: that unions should oppose the landowners' boycotts, with occupations if necessary, they they should press for a new law to expropriate all properties above forty, not just eighty hectares; that these should form large CERAs, as a means of effective planning; that this whole programme should come from initiatives from below, from the *campesino* councils. In terms of a class alliance we wanted to combine the full strength of the exploited — the workers, landless and smallest owners — against even the middle bourgeoisie, whom the Communists wanted to conciliate. We believed that such conciliation would prejudice any effective planning, not just the prospect of socialism.

Towards a revolutionary strategy: land occupations, the CERAs and the rise of the campesino *councils*

The work of unionization brought these questions to the fore. The only left-wing confederation of rural unions was Ranquil, controlled by the Communist and Socialist parties.

They urged the unions to align with the CUT and with their conciliation of the medium-size owners who, as we saw it, would never accept their overtures anyway. These meant, for example, that the unions shouldn't challenge land-owners' boycotts on production; that occupations should be discouraged, and less emphasis placed on CERAs and genuine participation by the *campesino* councils. Whereas we argued that conciliatory unionism was a gift for the Christian Democrats — as their policy was also reformist, new unions still joined their confederations. This seemed inevitable, unless we offered more drastic changes through *campesino* participation. So we did our best to put this across in our dealings with unionization.

This too meant hours of talking to *campesino* leaders. Our eventual plan was to found a new confederation to press for a revolutionary programme. We didn't present this to *campesinos* in terms of the need for socialism for its own sake. We tried to show them that only these policies would bring practical results. For instance, if there were just conciliatory, sectional unions, instead of *campesino* councils — uniting smallholders, sharecroppers (*medieros*), wage-earners, *asentamientos* and CERAs — how could they press for their common interests? For a new school, say. For a road, or for the expropriation of a landowner diverting their water. For all of them real changes depended on collective pressure. We'd put it to them that the first step in this direction was a new confederation.

Once again we were supported by the comrades at Catemu. They took the initiative in proposing a local *campesino* council. Their leaders needed no persuasion, but they also had a practical case: they'd realized that only these policies would bring improvements — in their case a school and effective irrigation system. We always stressed this point in meetings, which these comrades continued arranging. Often the most important were with perhaps three or four union leaders. Generally they'd been elected not on a political basis, but because they were known and trusted by the other *campesinos*. To make headway with them, we had now to win their trust. The Catemu comrades helped us in this. They made the concrete issues central and the leaders went back and raised them in their unions.

By mid 1971 our case for the 'new agrarian reform' was winning over many of them, though formally they still belonged to the *Triunfo Campesino*. The same was happening in other provinces where the MAPU was strong. In 1971 the *Triunfo* held its congress at Chiloé in southern Chile, and our supporters spoke out together. They demanded expropriation of all holdings over forty hectares, and increased powers for the *campesino* councils. We'd known that these measures would never get through — the Christian Democrats opposed any further expropriations — but a third of the delegates walked out and formed a new confederation: Worker-*Campesino* Unity (*Confederación Unidad Obrero - Campesino*). Local federations were formed in each province, mostly under MAPU leadership. Ranquil's leaders reserved their judgement. They welcomed the Christian Democrats' setback, but were also aware of the implications for policies within the left.

We were now better able to raise our demands. The first was for the rapid completion of the programme for the expropriation of properties over eighty hectares. We differed from the MIR on this question. Their occupations, often of smaller properties, were too spontaneous and isolated. Since the land reform existed, the first requirement was to advance within the existing legal framework. This meant occupations, but only to pressure the state apparatus into a more effective approach over holdings due for expropriation. We wanted to prevent landowners from evading reform by sub-dividing and intimidating their workers; to ensure that neighbouring holdings were expropriated jointly and converted into productive CERAs. Otherwise there could be little coordinated planning.

Our provincial federation was called 'Liberty and Progress'. It first planned its demands for expropriations.

These would be backed with occupations if necessary — as proved the case, since the CORA bureaucracy still resisted popular pressure. The Catemu smallholders and unions launched the first of these occupations, under the federation's direction.

The properties were selected on the basis of size and working conditions. We also stressed that their joint expropriation would facilitate local planning. The land-owners had already reacted to this prospect by beating their workers and getting them gaoled on trumped-up charges. So one morning they woke up to find their properties occupied. The *campesinos* had closed all access, set up several Chilean flags and demanded official intervention. This meant that CORA and INDAP officials had to go and mediate between the owners and the *campesinos*. I was there in my official capacity, when one of the landowners arrived. The *campesinos* forbade him to enter. For perhaps the first time ever, one of them stood up and spoke before he did. 'You can't come in. We're occupying the property because you've been boycotting production and refusing us our rights. Now we'll work it for ourselves. We're demanding its expropriation. We won't be discussing it with you, except through the land-reform authorities.'

This really threw the landlord off balance. The most he'd ever been used to hear from a *campesino* was 'good morning sir', and here they were telling him to get lost. Although they abused their workers, landlords regarded them as children, and expected them to reciprocate with subservience and complete dependence. And suddenly, this. The landlord went purple, looked round and saw me and the others from INDAP. He must have thought that if he could deal with us, everything would return to normal. He went straight to his car and came running back with a revolver — he was a cousin of Pinochet, imagine the fury of someone like that being turned off his land by his own *campesinos*. He made no secret of his intentions, waving the revolver at us, shouting his head off. 'They're the ones, those agitators, they're the ones who've caused this trouble. The workers on this farm have always been loyal, and you've stirred them up, I'll kill you.' He was on the point of firing when three of his workers grabbed the revolver and threw him down. Now it was their turn to talk.

'You've had this coming to you, thinking you could exploit us for ever. You thought we were stupid, but we're not. If we seem so, that's your doing.' Then they handed him over to the police, as he was threatening to kill them now. This was nothing unique — *campesino* leaders and left-wing officials were constantly threatened by the landowners, and after the coup, of course, many were murdered.

Well, all these properties were rapidly expropriated, without the owners being able to sub-divide or run them down first. We went on to further occupations, all planned in the same way, some twelve altogether. These widened support for the federation and its programme. The Communist Party and Ranquil opposed them, because occupations were 'illegal', but this only made our position clearer, as the results were indisputable.

The main one was that the CERAs were a success in Aconcagua. Following expropriation the union leaders and INDAP officials got down to planning how to work the various farms together — the number of workers to be involved, which crops to grow, credits, marketing, electing a directorate etc. Unlike the *asentamientos*, CERAs abolished the boundaries of former holdings, and hence the various distinctions and privileges deriving from them. Above all they had no employees in the capitalist sense. A typical *asentamiento* would have, say, twenty members, with exclusive control of decisions and profits, and another twenty wage labourers, with no such rights — former temporary workers (*afuerinos*) full members' sons and so on. CERAs involved all these former categories on a strictly equal basis. Also, women had full voting rights, while they had none in *asentamientos*. The other aspect was economic. In our view the need to maintain production would be better served by this larger scale, collective system, and indeed it was. The CERAs were obliged to invest their profits and sell their products at official, not black-market prices. They brought equal benefits to all their members, to their region and to the economy generally.

Aconcagua wasn't typical, though. While CERAs were part of the PU's official programme, they were token where expropriations were bureaucratic and isolated. This prevented planning and made CERAs weak because their members had not been involved in collective action. As on the *asentamientos*, they produced inefficiently and sold their products on the black market, exclusively in their own interests. This happened especially in provinces where official support for them was lacking — those dominated by the Communist Party and its MAPU sympathizers, who subsequently formed the MOC. Their few CERAs drifted away from collective production, even sub-dividing the land, and made little investment. They also had discipline problems, with drink and absenteeism etc., because they lacked a collective ethos.

Also in these areas, and for the same political reasons, the *campesino* councils were weaker, and brought no pressure on the CERAs to operate in everyone's interests. The councils were also officially recognized as consultative bodies combining all the exploited sectors. Again, though, they were only effective where the reforms had been pushed from below by all these sectors. In other areas, they had only union delegates and existed almost only on paper. They were instruments of the bureaucracy, rather than a source of mass pressure for genuinely socialist measures.

In Aconcagua it was the unions belonging to our federation which were most active in the councils. These were organized in the following way, to maximize participation. Each council was based on a zone, with delegates from each type of unit — CERAs, *asentamientos*, unions and smallholders' associations — and local delegates, all elected. They met each month to discuss local problems, dealt with meanwhile by sub-committees: production, marketing, planning, credits and defence were the main ones. They also had a political commission. Delegates would report back to assemblies within their area or organization. Hence all these cooperated over matters of common interest, particularly local planning — schools, roads and water supplies and so on. The production front, for example, would seek advice on the best source of seeds and arrange to get them. They also exchanged ideas — for instance, the Catemu comrades took up a suggestion for processing citrus, instead of selling their fruit at low prices to profiteering middlemen.

Catemu was typical of how the councils originated from practical issues which took on a political meaning. The smallholders there had several problems which might have swung them against the PU, if it failed to offer any solutions. First, they had no local school — they got one through the council. They also had irrigation problems, because bigger landowners up the valley diverted the water. This too was solved, though not without a confrontation — but this strengthened commitment to the council. As in Cautin before 1970, they realized that unity was their one strength. You'd often hear *campesinos* say; 'There's so many of us, yet we're so weak — why?' They realized that the answer was their traditional fragmentation, and so we overcame it. The council united the different sectors, especially smallholders and wage-earners, which had never before combined against the same exploitative system.

Apart from Catemu, the wage-earners' unions were usually the vanguard on these issues. For instance, the irrigation problem was solved mainly by pressure from workers on the farms concerned, when the issue had been raised in the council. At first the big owners resisted, but the unions forced them to give way. This militancy aroused disagreement over the councils among the various political parties. The Communists argued that they were a form of parallelism — that they were competing with the government and the CUT. Our view was that they were strengthening the PU with popular pressure: that they would align it with popular interests, instead of reform and bureaucratism.

As the political crisis deepened, this offered a means of defending the government through a popular power structure, in which provincial councils — combining those of different zones — would link up with the industrial cordons. In Aconcagua a provincial council was formed by mid-1972. This combined nine local ones, with a membership of some five or six thousand. All of them were already prepared to defend the PU if necessary. To our mind the Communist Party's opposition to such popular organizations indicated its divorce from the base and its failure to grasp the problems of power.

In 1972 I left Aconcagua for Valparaiso, though I continued working in both. My transfer was a party decision. In Valparaiso province *campesino* organization was weak: its delegates to the Chiloé congress hadn't joined our confederation. Its CORA and INDAP offices were dominated by the Communist Party. A couple of councils did exist, but only on paper. They consisted merely of some union and *asentamiento* delegates, who never consulted with their base. They rarely met, and did little more than sanction bureaucratic decisions. There'd been no attempt to build an alliance including the sharecroppers and smallholders. This left them exposed to the propaganda of the right, which local officials were conciliating. Even unionization was still very low, because workers hadn't been mobilized properly. There had been few land occupations, and the whole province had only two CERAs.

This meant that smallholders, for example, were completely isolated. When I arrived, there had just been an earthquake. Many *campesinos'* houses had collapsed and they were living in appalling conditions. Some prefabricated houses had been sent for, but CORA and INDAP had failed to distribute most of them. In the absence of councils there was little pressure on them to do so. On many *asentamientos* full members had been rehoused, but the non-members were living in shacks. Being unorganized, most of those in this situation were unaware that others shared it.

I and a comrade in INDAP set about remedying this, suggesting to the *campesinos* the need for a grassroots organization to pressure the bureaucracy. The problem of the Communist Party's opposition to such organizations, in favour of subordination to the CUT, was the latter's weakness at the local level. We were insisting that this level was crucial, not only because of these practical problems, but as a base for the PU.

Within weeks, as we dealt with the housing problem, several new unions were formed. These went on to cooperate in forming *campesino* councils. These were elected by the base, instead of involving union officials, as did the two existing councils — officials who typically held their positions because of their influence in party circles. The first of these new councils were in Limache and Quilpue. Like those in Aconcagua, they demanded the final expropriation of all properties over eighty hectares. This was in order to incorporate them into their overall plans for their areas. CORA resisted these demands, which led again to land occupations. Once more these were carefully planned to include several neighbouring units, which would then form a CERA. The number of CERAs grew month by month, as did the *campesino* councils. By late 1972 they were setting the pace of agrarian reform throughout the province; the bureaucrats who had failed for so long had virtually no choice in the matter.

The result was that I was publicly denounced, and the comrade working with me sacked, since he was junior to me. Immediately the Limache council organized a mass protest. They seized the main road out of Limache and demanded his reinstatement, and a meeting with Jacques Chonchol, then Minister of Agriculture. He came and promised an inquiry, but this didn't satisfy them. One new leader of the

council, who until a few months ago had had almost no
political experience, got up and berated him. 'We know all
about the bureaucrats. We're not satisfied with an inquiry
unless we're represented on it. If you're a revolutionary and
this is a revolutionary government, how come everything
depends on bureaucrats who don't listen to us?' It was the
first demonstration on this scale in the area, hundreds of
campesinos were there, and Chonchol accepted their
demands. An inquiry was held in which they took part and
the comrade was reinstated. Shortly afterwards the local
head of INDAP was replaced by a comrade from the
MAPU.

Worker-campesino *unity: the bosses' strikes and popular power*

When six local councils had been formed in Valparaiso, a
provincial one was also established. Its office was in
Quillota. Reformists within the PU argued that all this was
divisive, but the opposite was the case. For example, many
asentamientos traditionally influenced by Christian Democrats — and hence opposed to the PU — joined the councils.
This won them over politically. The reason was simple.
Although the councils demanded that *asentamientos* should
improve their wage-labourers' conditions, they also brought
them the benefits of popular pressure. For instance, the
provincial council improved marketing and distribution.
With INDAP's help it began exporting new local products.
It also organized their sale from local councils to the urban
poblaciónes (popular neighbourhoods). This more than
outweighed the *asentamientos*' previous returns from selling
their products on the black market. Successes like this
convinced us still further of the PU's need to rely on its base
as a source of strength.

This was confirmed in Aconcagua and Valparaiso when
the lorry-owners' strike began. With INDAP's trucks at their
disposal and these marketing links already established, the

provincial councils maintained food supplies to the cities. The trucks hardly stopped throughout the strike. *Campesino* escorts gave them protection. At this stage they had the upper hand. Though the trucks were sometimes sabotaged or attacked on the road, they usually got through. These experiences also led the councils to take an increasingly vanguard position. They demanded that the PU commandeer the strikers' lorries and establish a state transport system.

The growth of *campesino* consciousness in this period was impressive. They grew sharply aware of the question of power. Following the first bosses' strike, they regularized their contacts with the urban workers and industrial cordons. Many distribution arrangements developed in the strike were maintained. The two sectors held regular consultations, political as well as practical. *Campesino* participation in the March 1973 elections was higher than it had ever been, especially in Aconcagua. Several left candidates were elected in previously Christian Democrat areas. At the same time the councils were making increasingly political demands. Their leaders held meetings everywhere, linking *campesinos'* concerns to the more basic political issues, especially the question of popular power.

We in the MAPU, together with the MIR and sections of the Socialist Party, made this question increasingly central. It was not utopian, but was based precisely on this new popular mobilization. By now most *campesinos* could see that real benefits depended on their own organization. The right's propaganda — that 'the Marxists wanted to take their land and make them work for the state for nothing' — was made ineffective by what they experienced.

Despite bitterness at the PU's failure to deal decisively with the *tancazo*, this mobilization continued right up to the coup. In the second bosses' strike, the right was far more militant — they could see that the PU was retreating. Yet the provincial councils' response and that of the cordons was far more developed than in 1972, especially in Valparaiso.

As Aconcagua is less urban, these links were less strong there. It's also more easily controlled, as the main road out of it goes through a gorge, which the striking lorry-owners blocked. In Valparaiso by this time, though, there were communal commands which combined the councils and industrial cordons into a single working structure. This was what we had always aimed for, in naming our confederation 'Worker-*Campesino* Unity'. Between the two strikes the cordons' workers had helped the councils' land occupations, and the councils had supplied food to workers occupying factories. In the second bosses' strike regular convoys were established between Quillota and the cordon Cordillera, in Valparaiso. Workers helped to protect these convoys, which took food to the cordon and manufactures back to Quillota.

By now the government's attempts at a deal with the Christian Democrats were strengthening the right enormously. Attacks on the convoys became increasingly open and violent. Roads were blocked, though the *campesinos* often removed the lorries with tractors. On one occasion the lorry-owners fired on one of our trucks and killed the driver. Then they turned it over and set it on fire, with a wounded comrade still inside it. In Quillota the *campesinos* protested, demanding action from the PU and arms and new powers for the popular organizations.

Although we recognized to the end that factory workers were the vanguard, the *campesinos* were also central to this struggle. In some ways they were even firmer than factory workers. Less involved in traditional political structures, they tended to go straight to the point in these situations of confrontation — to think not of compromise, but of how to take a firm decision. In several joint meetings of the communal commands, it was they who inspired decisions when the others were still hesitating. The left must realize that the *campesinos* are fundamental to the revolution in Latin America, within a proletarian alliance.

The councils were increasingly clear about the solution to the crisis. They talked in terms of a popular power through which the masses would take decisions and also provide a defensive system. The plan was for a provincial command which would be elected in its own right from councils and cordons throughout the province. Above all, it would have new powers to defend the government.

The problems was that the government was not consulting with the masses, but with the right. It was buying time and abandoning power, without a struggle.

The reaction: the coup and the campesinos

This meant that despite our mobilization, the tide began to turn against us. Organized terrorism was launched against *campesino* councils. The police no longer intervened, and the *campesinos* had few weapons.

After the *tancazo*, for instance, when *campesinos* occupied farms near Quillota which were boycotting production, they were attacked by groups from the fascist Fatherland and Freedom Party. They were armed with machine guns. I was there when they attacked, at midnight, as the police were changing shifts. It was obviously fixed — the first shift left before the other one came to replace them. The *campesinos*, like the workers in the cities, felt increasingly isolated, except from one another. Without arms, they could make little even of this solidarity. On 4 September they staged a massive demonstration in support of the sailors detained by the navy for having denounced the plans for the coup. The president of the provincial council spoke at this meeting, demanding again that the PU should allow the people to defend it. Demonstrations continued throughout that week in Limache. By now they were regularly under attack, but they refused to be dispersed.

The coup was efficient. I was in Limache. By dawn on the eleventh all communications were cut and the town was surrounded. Two *campesino* comrades came to take me into hiding. One of them kept me in his home for several days. He kept repeating: 'How could the PU have ignored us when we were ready to defend them?' Everything had been prepared, but the party's orders never reached us.

Four days later I was back in Limache when I was trapped in a house-to-house search. It was the beginning of a year of torture in gaols and concentration camps. From one of them up in the Sierra I could see an *asentamiento* where they'd got new houses after the earthquake. I used to wonder what was happening there, as we had no news of the outside world.

My only contact with the *campesinos* was with a leader from one of the councils. He was with me in *La Legua*, one of the boats they use for prisoners in Valparaiso. He'd only become an activist a few months before the coup, and was completely disoriented by the torture, half out of his mind, unclear what was happening. We were next to one another in the hold. But as he began to get used to it, he gradually recovered his senses. We and other comrades began to talk. About the past, about the future. Even in the hold of *La Legua*, new cells were being formed.

PART III

SHANTYTOWNS

Background

Most large Latin American cities combine extremes of wealth and poverty. The latter is heavily concentrated in the shantytowns on their outskirts, where much of the low-income population lives in improvised housing, without sanitation, schools or basic medical services. The houses are built initially of waste material. They rarely have more than one or two rooms and often accommodate more than one family.

In Chile these areas are referred to either as *poblaciónes* ('neighbourhoods'), *callampas* ('mushrooms', in cases where they sprang up suddenly) or *campamentos* ('encampments'). The latter are settlements with a relatively high degree of organization in defence of their rights, usually inspired by politicians. (Because of these special connotations, the term *'campamento'* is left in Spanish throughout this chapter.)

Piecemeal solutions to these conditions have been offered by reformist governments in most Latin American countries but with little success. Only in Cuba have they been abolished. The Christian Democrats in Chile established limited housing programmes and neighbourhood associations (*juntas de vecinos*), but in spite of this the shantytowns grew in the 1960s.

This was inevitable, in that the fundamental problem was not just housing, but poverty in general. Though many conventionally employed workers live in shantytowns, due to low wages, a large proportion of their inhabitants are either under-employed or unemployed, as industrial growth in Latin America does little to increase employment; the companies involved are for the most part multi-nationals with a small and specialized work force. In these circumstances, shantytowns are the only outlet for most of the low-income population. Despite the conditions, their urban setting is generally preferred to the rural one from which many of their occupants come.

Their problems have nevertheless become an increasingly political issue, as left-wing parties recognized the growing discontent in these areas. In Chile under the Christian Democrats many of them launched their own campaigns for local improvements. Encouraged by the left-wing parties, they developed their own forms of struggle, notably the land occupations and patterns of internal organization by virtue of which they came to be known as *campamentos*. Their names — *Nueva la Habana* (New Havana), Lenin, Ho Chi Minh — reflected their growing political awareness. These largely autonomous developments continued into the PU period, despite the much greater official provision for economic and social improvements.

Foremost among the left-wing parties concerned with this sector was the MIR, partly because its recent and substantially student origins limited its penetration of the organized labour movement. New Havana, where Laura was active as a member of the MIR, was closely associated with it. As she admits, its high degree of organization and political awareness was untypical. Nevertheless, it expressed a potential which raises fundamental questions about this increasingly large sector in Latin America today. Who are its inhabitants, in class terms, and what can they offer to the struggle in which all sectors of the left are agreed that the working class proper is the vanguard? In the lorry-owners' strikes, for example, neighbourhood organizations were crucial in maintaining distribution. The MIR, especially, stressed the importance of building relations between *campamentos* and industrial cordons, in the form of the communal commands which developed as the crisis mounted. The Communist Party saw them as less important, given their lack of the cohesion involved in relationships in the work-place, as opposed to those of residence.

Today New Havana has ironically been renamed 'New Dawn' by the military junta. Its leaders have been tortured and executed and its eight thousand inhabitants terrorized. Many of them have had to leave, and those who remain are close to starvation. These new conditions can only have sharpened the awareness which the previous period gave them, reiterating the question of their political importance.

6
A Mobilized Shantytown:
New Havana

Speaker: LAURA, 24, member of the MIR, who was active in the *campamento* New Havana (*Nueva la Habana*)

The origins of New Havana

During the Popular Unity period I was politically active in New Havana, a Santiago *campamento* organized mainly by the MIR. The *campamentos* are poor housing areas on the fringes of the major cities. They consist mainly of one-room shacks with very little sanitation, running water or electricity. They're distinct from the *poblaciónes*, or traditional shantytowns, in being somewhat organized. This is usually on a political basis dating from the land occupations which first brought them into being.

Their roots thus lie in the housing shortage common to most South American cities. It's widely assumed that most people in them are unemployed immigrants from the country, but this is only part of the story. In New Havana many people were regular workers, though typically with unstable jobs, in construction for instance. The point is that the living conditions in these areas aren't unusual — they're shared by much of the working class, not just the under-employed or unemployed.

Previously these people lived mainly in the *conventillos*,

big, old houses in the city centre, where whole families occupy single rooms. In such conditions, and with rising rents, they became very militant about housing. This led them to organize land occupations, especially in the late 1960s under the Christian Democrat government. In this way they hoped to obtain their own houses. The Christian Democrats tried to keep up with this mass movement by setting up neighbourhood associations. But like everything else these land occupations outran their reforms to the point where they were beyond their control.

The MIR had strong support in these areas. We began our mass work with them in the late 1960s, as with the poorer *campesinos*. We had several reasons for attaching special importance to them. Workers as such — in their place of work — were dominated by the traditional left-wing parties. We had little chance of competing with them. The shantytowns, with their mixed population, including the city's poorest people, were much more accessible to us. For one thing the housing problem is perhaps the most obvious contradiction of capitalism in Latin America, and the most persistent. For another, it was common to all those who lived there — factory workers, small shopkeepers, street-sellers, craftsmen. The *campamento* was in itself a means of bringing these groups together.

Our scope increased when the Christian Democrats' housing reforms were swept aside by the land occupations. The ones which developed into New Havana were almost the first in Santiago — one on a university site, another on a private holding, the third on church land. The Christian Democrats panicked and tried to repress this so-called 'movement of the homeless' with riot squads. This only raised people's determination. In what became New Havana, for instance, two participants were killed, and the riot squad kept prowling about and firing in the air to scare people. Meantime most of them were still living in shelters made of old cartons and rags, whatever anyone could find.

Such experience sowed the seeds of their internal organization. They formed their own militias to defend themselves
from the riot squad. There was also a health front to care
for the wounded — they couldn't go to hospital, because
they would have been arrested.

As well as working with these communities we helped to
create some, by setting up 'committees of the homeless'.
Sometimes they consisted of a group of neighbours living in
rented accommodation; others developed among employees
of the same firm or government department, some among
the armed forces even. These committees took part in the
land occupations, which were usually overnight. The MIR
was involved in many of those in the second half of 1970,
when there were three hundred just in the capital, Santiago.
The repression was violent, reaching its height with the
Puente Alto occupation, when several people were killed.
But once the election was under way, the Christian
Democrats had to drop this. The land occupations now met
little opposition.

At this point three of those led by the MIR, and involving
about eight thousand people, combined to demand a new
place to live. The Christian Democrats, eager for votes, gave
them some land called 'La Florida', on the outskirts of
Santiago. They promptly renamed it 'New Havana'. Its
development was vital to us. We were still a clandestine
organization centred in the universities. New Havana was
one of our first mass fronts.

The MIR's strategy in this sector was different from that
of the other left parties. They also organized land
occupations, but mainly for votes. Our goal was long-term
mobilization. We saw this as a central part of our transition
to mass action. And of course our broad strategy at this
stage was insurrectionary, not electoral. In New Havana
the organization originally designed for the occupations
developed into a permanent structure. For us it was the
embryo of a lasting political experiment.

The internal structure of the campamento

The *campamento* had three main fronts, all dating from the occupations. The cultural one, concerned with leisure and propaganda, the health front and the defensive militias. Sub-divided into brigades, these militias were subject to popular assemblies, which also elected new members to them. The brigade commanders worked together as the directorate of the militias. They dealt not only with physical threats to the *campamento*, but also with internal security and with disciplinary matters like disputes between neighbours. In the early stages their role was central.

However, the militias couldn't provide for our long-term organizational needs. Originally they were the vanguard, our only defence against the daily threats from the riot squads. They were still important in the 1970 elections, when we gave Allende our critical support and there was danger of a coup. With the PU in power, though, the repression and the danger subsided. We turned our thoughts to a permanent structure for the *campamento*.

The decisions involved were made by the popular assembly, though most proposals did come from the activists in the *campamento*. First a directorate was set up. Originally there'd been one in each of the three occupations, but these now merged. This reflected reorganization at the base, where the key unit was the *manzana*, a block of roughly forty houses. Each *manzana* had its own assembly, meeting once or twice a week, where *campamento* affairs were discussed. Each of these in turn sent a delegate to the directorate. Finally, there was an inner directorate of seven persons, directly elected by everyone in the *campamento*. This was the core of the leadership. Meantime the militias were replaced by perimeter guards for the *campamento*, a security front for internal defence and a disciplinary commission, to settle disputes and ensure proper conduct by comrades in office.

Most people in the directorate were active members of the MIR, but this structure wasn't imposed by the party. It developed itself and was highly organic, the local peoples' own response to what they'd lived through. This basis in collective experience was its main strength.

The cultural front

It was probably the cultural front which attracted most participation, although it went through quite a crisis in mid 1971. By this time New Havana was something of an attraction to intellectuals and artists, whose influence was almost fatal. For instance, at one of its meetings an intellectual from outside the *campamento* insisted that the cultural front should step up its political education. This idea was extraneous, for two reasons. First, local people already had a profound political education arising from their own experiences. Secondly, although many of them were politically active, they weren't necessarily interested in political debates by intellectuals. On this occasion a discussion on underdevelopment was launched. Most people at the meeting soon left. Only the visiting intellectuals and a few real activists stayed, the latter mainly out of politeness. Thereafter the cultural front declined — people lost interest because it wasn't answering their needs. In the end it was reconstituted as a coordinating.body for political mobilization and local educational programmes.

To take these first. The comrades set up a nursery school where working mothers could leave their children. They lobbied the educational department for the materials for a new school, which they then built, and refurbished buses for extra classrooms. A parent-teacher group was set up to discuss the way the schools were run, and children were represented. They produced some striking new ideas. Especially they challenged the assumption that classroom education was more important than experience. This debate with the teachers was a long one, but finally the classes did get a much more practical orientation. The children went on outings to the nearby foothills of the Andes for botany and biology classes. For mathematics they visited their parents' work-places to count the machines and learn about angles — and this taught them to respect what their parents were doing, in itself a minor revolution.

The effect on the teachers was very marked — most were from outside the *campamento*. Parents and children were now questioning many of the assumptions implicit in their traditional teaching. The teachers were gradually proletarianized. The way they spoke to the children, their demands that they arrive clean and tidy and spot on time, when their fathers might have kept them awake by getting drunk on the previous night — all this was now questioned. For the first time the teachers had to adapt to their working environment. Their own social education now went hand in hand with their teaching.

We also launched a literacy programme using the methods of Paulo Freire. Politically, it was an ideal time for Freire's combination of teaching people to read and write and also look critically at their environment. There were lengthy discussions about what were the most interesting and important words to learn, words like 'government', for instance. The illiteracy rate was very high, and the classes were organized by *manzana*. Very few people took part at first. This was partly because the classes were being held in the school, in the evenings. The adults were ashamed to be going to their own children's classrooms. So we transferred the classes to the *manzanas*. Far more people then took part. By the time the coup put an end to all this, illiteracy in New Havana was virtually a thing of the past.

We also organized leisure activities, song competitions and a youth theatre. This was especially successful. It performed in other *campamentos* and industrial cordons. Its biggest success was *The Story of the Land Occupation* based on local people's experiences. The children remembered these vividly and devised most of the play themselves. Even the smallest of them would say: 'Well, this is what I was doing then', and that's basically how it developed. The

six-to-ten age group presented it on the second anniversary
of the formation of New Havana. This was during the
bosses' strike of October 1972. It was striking how the kids'
perception of their elders helped to reinforce their unity,
which was so critical at this period. They completely
captured the character of the land occupations' original
leaders, even their ideological disputes — the way one
leader had demanded one thing, another something
different, and so on. The extent to which the militias' power
had gone to their heads, their swaggering style, the
domineering character of relationships between men and
women — they caught it all, from things they'd seen and
conversations they'd overheard. Somehow they put it all into
perspective, affirming that a new unity had eventually been
forged from it.

The health front and the campaign against alcoholism

This new awareness, even among children, showed itself in
many ways. For instance, there was one hopeless alcoholic in
the *campamento*, called Panchito. From having once been
teased, he became a kind of leader for them. Even when
drunk he was never violent — he used to dance and the
children danced with him. His only occupation was carving
and painting wooden flowers, and he taught them how to do
it. They came to respect and obey him, and I think it was
this which kept him stable, despite his drinking.

Alcoholism was common in New Havana, as elsewhere in
Chile. With generations of repression behind them, workers
drink heavily as a way of escaping from their problems. This
was a major concern of the health front. First it lobbied the
National Health Service to sponsor a local health organization — the government was supposed to send its own nurses
and doctors to New Havana, but they hardly ever came. In
the end we got permission for this, with a representative of
each *manzana* receiving training from the Health Service in
nursing and first aid etc. The comrade in charge of the

health front had a more intensive course, which even trained her for emergency operations. We also got a clinic, an ambulance and regular visits from a doctor. All this was the product of the health front's pressure on the Health Service, especially by women comrades.

Many women were also strongly committed to combating alcoholism. Drunken confrontations, when men came home at night, were frequent. Alcoholism was also a mainstay of male chauvinism (*machismo*). After drinking, men felt obliged to assert their authority over their wives, especially now that many women had social activities outside the home, in the *campamento*. This new independence caused some really violent scenes, especially on paydays, when drinking was always at its heaviest.

Our first step was to eliminate the dozens of small, illicit bars where most of this heavy drinking took place, at extortionate prices. The assembly succeeded in doing this. Just one survived — one stubborn character set up his bar at the very entrance to the *campamento*, with the wine right there in the window. It wasn't too successful, though, because anyone leaving it to come into the *campamento* was checked by the security front and detained if drunk. We were apprehensive about possible reactions to this, but there was surprisingly little resistance. Our long-term solution was to increase alcoholics' involvement in the life of the *campamento*. We'd encourage them to come home early, for instance, and join in their *manzana* assembly. By these means, and by professional medical treatment, some eighty or so comrades were cured of varying degrees of alcoholism.

This had a visible effect on the everyday life of the *campamento*. You could now go out at three or four in the morning, with little danger of being molested. I often had to, and never had problems. Outside New Havana it was immediately different — any woman out late in a shanty-town was likely to run into trouble with drinkers. But in New Havana, no. You were safe.

Mobilization and participation: the role of women and young people

Mass participation in all these activities was crucial. They taught much more than political harangues, and anyway little could be achieved without popular pressure on the bureaucracy. We had to mount demonstrations to get housing materials, health facilities etc. People also had to be involved in the *campamento's* security system — within a few months of the PU's election, the repression was creeping back. The riot squads appeared again, especially at demonstrations, and the only thing which kept them at bay was the level of popular mobilization. People had a tremendous pride in belonging to the *campamento*, and they showed it on demonstrations — when they arrived, the people from other *campamentos* used to shout: 'They're here, they're here!'

Elsewhere, of course, reactions were different. The New Havana people were known as 'the delinquents' to the right-wingers, who were often terrified of them — they were just too used to assuming that shantytown dwellers would always be humble. One confrontation showed especially the difference which grassroots pressure could make. The local mayor was very right-wing, and always harassing the *campamento*. Sometimes he'd cut off the electricity, at other times the water supply, and often the rubbish wasn't cleared. The carts were supposed to come every two days, but once they were missing for a week. It was summer, the stench and flies everywhere. The *manzanas* brought this up in the assembly, which produced a plan of action. Two large trucks were filled with rubbish, and we hoisted the *campamento's* flags on them. Off we went, with a New Havana security command in front and half the *campamento* following, to the municipal offices. When officials refused to open the gates, we drove the trucks through them. Everyone took a hand in dumping the rubbish in the mayor's office. From then on the rubbish trucks were sent to New Havana daily.

Women were prominent in all these activities, whereas in other *campamentos* there were special women's sections which precluded participation on equal terms. In New Havana there was real integration; in the directorate, on the marches, even in the confrontations. The driver of the clinic's ambulance, which operated at night, was a woman. Women virtually ran the health front. They helped guard the *campamento* at night. Sometimes the husband would attend *manzana* meetings, sometimes the wife, if possible, both. This weakened male chauvinism at a very basic level.

Of course there was lots of resistance to this — cases of husbands forbidding wives to go to meetings, and drinking and beating them up if they did so. The assembly dealt with such cases. Its reprimands had some effect, but on the whole in this short space of time, traditional attitudes held the day. The real change was among young people. For instance, in their play on the story of the land occupation, they realized how prominent women had been. Young people also took part together in new occupations of schools, factories and land. When the girls stood up as well as the boys to confrontations, they became very much just comrades, not 'boys' and 'girls' in the narrow sense.

Talking of the young, even children played their part in the *campamento*. Through the youth front they took part in building houses, demonstrations and even in the assembly on subjects affecting them, like schooling. They also helped guard the *campamento*, especially at times when adults were scarce, like during local fiestas. They made the most of our demonstration banners, and in the 1972 stoppage, they helped maintain local distribution. One shrimp of a kid invariably led our slogan-chanting in the major demonstrations. *'Campamento'*, he'd shout: and the others would answer, *'Nueva la Habana'*. 'Ché Guevara', everyone called him, he wouldn't be known by any other name. The adults were proud of their children's involvement.

The effects of this could also be seen on an everyday level. In shantytowns the kids spend most of their time in gangs.

These are often virtual teenage mafias. They're unapproachable, aggressive, and also make life very dangerous at night. In New Havana this simply died out. Only young adults who'd previously been delinquents still occasionally had relapses. We also had one special case of a teenager who was semi-delinquent. He was an orphan, extroverted and a good singer, and he always got other kids to follow him. He didn't have any time for school and just ran wild. But we won him round by giving him the chance to sing at *campamento* concerts. He began to take notice of us and take part. We treated him as a little adult, and in return he became a comrade and organizer of many of the children's activities.

Like the adults, few young people had time for political discussions. With concrete tasks, though, it was different. For instance they were fully in charge of the *campamento's* fire precautions. The whole fire-fighting front consisted of sixteen to eighteen-year-olds, and they always dealt competently with fires.

Not surprisingly, these young people acquired quite a status with the young in other *campamentos*. Their political awareness was much higher. Whenever I was with them elsewhere, at football matches for example, I noticed the respect this won them, and how it influenced other young people into similar activities.

Security and people's justice: the seeds of an autonomous system

We still had serious security problems after disbanding the militias. Defence of the *campamento* itself was undertaken by popular guards, with each *manzana* responsible for one night, in rota. One adult from each of the forty households per *manzana* would take part, usually the man, but sometimes the woman — it was left to each family to settle this. The guards were stationed at each of the three main entrances, armed with sticks, never with firearms. In the event of anything suspicious — including at times right-wing attacks — they would raise the alarm. People entering after midnight had to identify themselves. Anyone drunk was handed on to the security front, which was in charge of internal order. This also had people on duty each night at its headquarters, in the centre of the *campamento*. Any non-resident was thoroughly checked and his documents held until he left. In this way we foiled several attacks by the fascist Fatherland and Freedom Party.

Our security also depended on the maintenance of internal cohesion. Out of this need there grew the beginnings of a system of popular justice, distinct not just from the bourgeois courts, but from bourgeois legality itself. Those three years were too short and turbulent for this to acquire a definitive form, but there were real steps towards it.

These experiments also had their roots in the original land occupations, in the need for unity which they entailed. The constant threat of repression gave rise in effect to new types of offence — acts of betrayal or carelessness, which might weaken our defences. At first the militias dealt with such cases. Generally simple collective pressure would convince the offender of the social danger of his action, in view of the struggle then in progress. Expulsion from the *campamento* was used only in exceptional cases.

With the *campamento* established and the PU in power, the problems were different. Although the physical threat was less, the need for a genuine people's justice was more obvious than ever, as we still had a bourgeois judicial system. It had little concern with the *campamento's* real interests. We needed independent solutions for problems like speculation and hoarding. How to provide them? The militias' disciplinary powers had been an improvised crisis measure. What sort of structure should replace them?

Though we never really answered this question, we did go beyond the PU's version of neighbourhood courts (*tribunales vecinales*). These operated, especially in Communist-led

campamentos, as adjuncts of the bourgeois courts, to deal
with mild local offences like petty theft. They still neglected
the basic problem of redefining the class-ridden notion of
what was 'illegal'. Instead they just delegated an already
existing system, reinforcing all its values. In fact these courts
usually died out, because they simply didn't provide for the
problems which concerned people most.

In New Havana we did attempt to provide for new needs.
Not only did we deal locally with the traditional petty
offences, but we also covered new ones, defined as such by
the assembly: for instance, officiousness or neglect by
members of the directorate, or infringement of our rules on
hygiene. This allowed a constant response to new problems
like hoarding and the black market, particularly.

So much for the scope. But we still had the problem of a
structure for this new popular justice — who would take
part and exactly how, and what sort of penalties would be
imposed. In these respects we were improvising right up to
the time of the coup. Most cases were dealt with by the
directorate or the relevant *manzana*, depending on their
importance. Family disputes were settled at *manzana* level,
with socially useful penalties, like cleaning the *manzana* or
digging new drains. The number of cases which had to go to
a higher level was very few. This was sometimes for
traditional reasons — a woman might prove reluctant to
testify against her husband — but also because the
incidence of more important problems declined when
people knew that they could be dealt with, ultimately by the
assembly. So there were the seeds of an effective popular
justice.

Inevitably we were faced increasingly with political
problems — political misconduct, speculation by traders
and so on. These were referred to the directorate, which
submitted its decisions to the assembly. We tried to find
positive solutions, by matching the penalties to the needs of
the *campamento* — typically, street cleaning. Failing this,
offenders were expelled. This came to a head with the

problems posed by the lorry-owners' and bosses' strike in October 1972.

The bosses' strikes: maintaining supplies and distribution

In New Havana small shopkeepers controlled distribution. Most of them were extortionists, although they did provide some employment. Within the *campamento* there were roughly a hundred and fifty of them. People's purchasing on a small scale — the only one they could afford — increased the scope for profiteering.

The official means of regulating supplies and prices were the JAPs, promoted mainly by the Communist Party. In New Havana we tried instead for an understanding with the shopkeepers. They agreed to buy from official sources and also to sell at official prices. This would leave them a reasonable profit and prevent hoarding and black marketing. Like the JAPs this had little success, and for much the same reason: the penalties were weak and hard to enforce. Congress rejected Allende's proposals for strengthening them, and the Judiciary hardly applied them, because it was also controlled by the right. So what penalty could the people impose, either with or without the JAPs? In highly organized *campamentos* like New Havana, offending shopkeepers could be expelled. But this was only a local solution, as they then set up in other areas where people were more easily exploited. The assembly was always discussing this problem. It reflected the PU's weak control in this case of the distributive system, which it was reluctant to really challenge for fear of a right-wing reaction. Our local problems were those of Chile as a whole, of the PU's limited power and programme.

By early 1973, with the shortage caused by the lorry-owners' strike, the shopkeepers were holding people to ransom. Despite our efforts to be patient, most of them kept up their old ways. Our only solution was to force them to close. And so instead we relied on a 'people's store'

(*Almacén Popular*). This was set up with contributions from the *manzanas*, while the State gave us credit for a stock of supplies. By selling at official prices, this acquired a virtual monopoly of non-perishable goods. This confined the shopkeepers to perishables, which made hoarding and speculation harder. The store belonged to the *campamento* and was managed by the directorate. As it extended its operations and put the small shopkeepers out of business, they were given first choice of becoming its salaried employees. This provided some conciliation, kept them in work and put their expertise to good use.

By these means we kept living standards in the *campamento* rising. For instance the houses, which were wooden and prefabricated, began with bare floors. By the end of three years almost all the floors were covered. Also most families began with only one bed between them, but by 1973 they managed to buy separate ones, and blankets. There was even a communal television in most *manzanas*.

Despite all these measures the second stoppage in mid 1973 created serious shortages. At this point the government supplemented the people's store by sending supplies to the *campamento* for direct sale at official prices. Meanwhile the directorate set up a successful rationing system, which ensured that everyone got their share, according to the size of their family. We also arranged direct supplies by contacting *campesino* councils and hiring trucks to purchase supplies from them. These were sold at a 'people's market' (*Mercado Popular*) which the directorate also ran, again with a rationing system to ensure equal distribution.

All these problems had two levels. While forced to confront them in terms of day-to-day survival, we were equally aware of the need for a fundamental solution to them. In our view this could be only an overall structure of popular power to which New Havana would belong. We were well aware of the limitations of changes within one *campamento*. In the bosses' strikes we stressed the importance of widening the industrial cordons into communal commands. These would include the *campa-mentos* and *campesinos* and serve as an embryonic alternative to the bourgeois state apparatus.

Together with the revolutionary wings of MAPU and the Socialist Party, we worked for the transformation of the nearby Vicuña Mackenna cordon into a communal command including the New Havana area. We recognized that the cordon, with its industrial workers, would be the vanguard of this structure. In the bosses' strikes the two areas achieved a number of joint actions such as factory occupations and distribution measures. It was also through this new structure that we did our best to prepare for the coup — but, as it turned out, time was against us.

The coup: the dispersal and legacy of New Havana

New Havana paid for its reputation. The military and the bourgeoisie had a special hatred for the people there because they were known not just for their words, but for their actions. Whenever they said they were going to take action, they really went ahead and took it. The almost legendary status this gave them was treated as a crime, deserving a specially brutal repression.

For the same reason the *campamento* came under attack by groups of fascists before the coup. Infiltration was always a problem and in October 1972, with our mobilization against the strike, threats were made against us daily. Luckily we'd just doubled our guards when the first attack came, at one in the morning. Two buses drew up at the entrance and about a hundred figures poured out. They were dressed in the white cloaks of the fascist Fatherland and Freedom Party. The alarm bell was immediately rung, rousing the whole *campamento*. Luckily most activists were just on their way back from meetings. Although we were armed only with sticks, the fascists turned tail, firing a few shots, as soon as they saw us. Later there were other attacks, often in answer to our anti-fascist demonstrations.

Though they raised our morale, these confrontations were also a warning to the right of the *campamentos'* defensive capacity. In the final months before the coup this developed strongly. Ten women's brigades were formed, for instance, to provide first aid and play a key defensive role. The plan was for liberated zones, of which New Havana would have been one, to support the main resistance fronts. Each would have a first aid centre and serve as a central source of supplies as well as having its own defence system. Provision was made for removing the elder women and children and combining with neighbouring *campamentos*. So locally, at least, we were reasonably prepared. The problem was that the revolutionary left as a whole was taken by surprise in a tactical sense, not by the occurrence of the coup, but by its timing. Our information was that we had at least a week in hand. In the event we had few resources for resisting in the *campamento*. In any case the overall scheme wasn't fully prepared, partly because of the recent arms searches and the repression that came with them.

We did our best, though. At eight in the morning, when we heard of the coup, the directorate went underground, while some brigades went to Vicuña Mackenna and Puente Alto. Both areas resisted for several days. The fact is, though, that the coup was efficient. The military inadequacy of the left reflected its political weakness and indecision. In the first few hours the resistance's basic structure was broken by the arrests and executions and the cutting of communications. The MIR's radio station was the first to be captured, at 7.30, and one by one the others followed. Even the telephones were out of action. The only means of communicating was by walky-talky and ham radios. The truth is that we never expected such ruthlessness as the bombing of the Moneda Palace, nor the military's technical efficiency — a serious mistake on our part, but something which also convinces me that US technicians were directly involved.

The repression inflicted on the *campamento* was

apparently meant to eliminate every trace of what happened in those three years. They even changed its name to 'New Dawn'. Several other *campamentos* have been given the names of generals. Within hours of the coup, the military began random attacks on New Havana which continued right up to the time I left Chile. The first occurred on the night of 11 September. They simply went into the *manzanas*, took the first sixteen men they found and shot them immediately in the main square. One day it was the army, the next the navy, the next the police — sometimes there were four or five searches a day. Women were raped in front of their men, and children beaten in front of their parents. Almost every home they went into was sacked — and this cut deep, because our programme for improving the houses was due to be completed by December. It was as if the two joint struggles for new homes and socialism were both being destroyed together. Every morning there'd be fresh bodies at the entrance of the street between New Havana and the neighbouring *campamento*. They were clearly left there deliberately, to terrify people.

Even so they resisted as best they could. The activists in the *campamento* were known to almost everyone, their identity if not their hideouts. But no one denounced them, even under torture. One woman who wasn't an activist, just a sympathizer, had both arms broken, but we know for a fact that she didn't give any information. Once they tortured six comrades together, right there in the *campamento*, but again they gave nothing away. When we left a few weeks later, the *campamento's* whole leadership was still intact.

Already, though, the *campamento* was breaking up. Dozens of families were leaving, some from fear, many from hunger. Others refused to remain in the area after the military renamed it. Every day you'd see people departing, mostly for relatives in the country, with handcarts filled with what belongings they had left.

Given the nature of the coup, the *campamento*, as it had

become was bound to be eradicated. In fact, we'd long been asking ourselves whether what we were doing in New Havana was realistic at this stage. We'd come to feel that our concern with its internal organization was perhaps over-concentrated. One thing the coup has shown is that even the so-called sub-proletariat can't be won over by fascism when they've had an experience like New Havana. But in present circumstances, the struggle does lie more clearly than ever with the workers in their factories. Though there were such people in New Havana, the basis of our unity there, over housing, now belongs to the past.

This doesn't mean that New Havana was in vain. Several thousand people from there have joined the resistance on other fronts, including key ones, like Vicuña Mackenna. Their struggle wasn't a central one, but their experience belongs to the future. The further they scatter those who shared it, the more its effect will multiply.

PART IV

THE UNIVERSITIES

Background

Like all South American universities, Chile's in 1970 reflected the ruling-class's dependence on European and North American ideologies and culture. They bore little relation to local requirements, either technical or social. Their medical schools, for example, were as much concerned with heart transplants as with infant mortality. Technical training contributed little to the need for popular consumer goods or technological independence in areas like copper production. Also inadequate public schooling restricted university entrance to those who could pay for supplementary private teaching.

Student movements have nevertheless been a radical force in Latin America. Questioning first the dominance of the traditional oligarchies, they became strongly nationalist in the 1940s and 1950s. After the Cuban revolution this nationalism grew increasingly left-wing. Chile was no exception. Under Frei students won reforms which allowed them a significant part in university administration. By 1970 their support for Allende was strong, in the expectation that universities would be deeply involved in the changes promised by the PU.

Its formula was that the universities should be 'at the service of Chilean society'. Teaching would cater for Chilean needs, and students would contribute to the development of the country, through technical studies and voluntary labour. Entrance would be open to students who hadn't been able to afford preparation for university entrance. An agreement was made with the CUT for extension courses in the unions.

All these proposals were implemented. New courses developed and traditional ones changed. Thousands of students did voluntary work in development projects. Technical students did applied research in the factories, mines and agrarian reform centres. The universities helped to make cheap editions of the classics available to a mass public. Their own research and publications on Chilean society became integral to the social policies which the PU implemented.

Meanwhile student politics reflected those of the wider society. Student support for the PU grew, but then as polarization deepened university departments became increasingly divided. The left was weakened by the absence of staff on government secondment and the return of Christian Democrats seconded before 1970. Also, each year's new student intake injected into the university the increasingly right-wing views of the average student's middle-class parents. Early in 1972 the PU candidate lost the election for rector of the University of Chile. The opposition now took the offensive. Eventually confrontations brought university life to a standstill, with the fascist Fatherland and Freedom Party influencing the centrist opposition of Christian Democrat students and teachers.

Raul's opinion, as a student leader and Communist Party activist, was that left-wing students should concentrate on supporting the PU's programme within the university. For him the left's demise was due largely to other left parties' excessive demands and to their student activists working on fronts outside the university, which they considered more important.

In many universities, resistance to the coup was strong. Students and university teachers have since been heavily repressed, but continue to play a central part in popular resistance to the junta.

7
The Students' Polarization
in the University of Chile

Speaker: RAUL, 22, activist of the Communist Party and student leader in the state University of Chile, in Santiago

Student politics: the campaign of 1970

Throughout the PU period I was a student activist in the University of Chile. It was always a political weather-vane, an indicator of the direction in which the balance of power was moving. In the late 1960s its radicalization produced massive support for the PU in the 1970 election. Then under the PU, its ultra-leftism, to my way of thinking and that of other party comrades, was symptomatic of the polarization which ended in the PU's downfall.

In 1968, under Frei, a university reform was passed after years of militant pressure from students. This gave them far greater participation in the running of the universities. The next year the left gained control from the Christian Democrats of the national students' union (*Federación de Estudiantes de Chile*). The Christian Democrats' youth section sympathized heavily with the PU and many of them came over to it. It was in this same year that I was elected as a student leader in Santiago.

Previously I'd been active in a group of the ultra-left, but after the election it divided, and went mainly to the

Communist Party. The PU's victory, for which we'd campaigned, convinced us that we should be working within the mass parties of the left, now that Allende was in power. I don't think this was the abandoning of an immature position. For me it was primarily a response to a changed political situation. Previously we'd been working clandestinely with a view to armed insurrection and concentrating our propaganda on workers untouched by the main left-wing parties, especially in small, non-unionized copper mines. This no longer made sense. In 1970 there was a new and, at that moment, a more real way forward, which we recognized as such and supported.

At the time of the election I was still formally in this group, so that my activities were only partly in the University. But already as a student leader I was involved with other students in campaigning for Allende in Santiago. With the PU parties already dominant among them, many were active day and night for weeks before the actual election. In the morning there'd be mass meetings focused at first on political discussion, and later on planning the day's campaigning outside the University. This consisted in visiting the shantytowns and other residential areas to hold discussions and mass meetings and campaign from door to door — outlining the PU's programme, what it would mean for people living there, answering their questions about it.

We also had propaganda brigades to go out and paint every available wall with slogans and political pictures. Though it's hard for Europeans to imagine, this is standard electoral practice in Chile, and especially important for the left, as the right controls the conventional media. It's also an indication to voters of the relative strength of the right and left, as both are active in it. This means it's also a battleground. Propaganda brigades would be out every night, and when they met there were often armed clashes. These were usually started by the right, by firing at us from passing cars. Although they were much better equipped, they had to use these methods because they were far less expert at thinking up slogans and at painting. Another difference was that the right often hired its painters and armed them with guns as well as brushes, while on the left only activists painted.

The results of these confrontations were encouraging. The right became very hit-and-run, because of the mass support we had. We could feel it growing daily. Our victory on the walls was an omen of the polls. By election day we were sure we would win, though apprehensive about right-wing reactions. As results came through in the evening and through the night of 4 September, complete euphoria took over, first in the university and then in the streets of Santiago, where we all went out to join it. People sang and danced in every square, oblivious of who were students, workers, housewives or whatever, aware of one thing only, that they were all of the left, which had won. That night, for once, the right stayed at home. It was as if socialism had already been established — though we'd soon discover that there was rather more to this than winning a victory at the polls.

The impact of the PU: the University and the transition towards socialism

The universities took on a new role with the PU in power. Its purpose was to put them at the service of a changing Chilean society. This idea had long been voiced by students, but now it was possible to apply it.

The basic changes were as follows. First it was made much easier for people from working-class families, and in some cases workers themselves, to study at the university. Secondly, the content of courses changed: problems were seen in more socialist terms, and designed to make practical contributions to Chile's economic independence. Finally practice was built into theory — students now had to spend part of their time applying the skills which they were learning, as an integral part of their courses.

I was personally involved in these changes in the Faculty of Engineering, as a student member of its planning committee. The most important alterations were in mining engineering, as copper is Chile's biggest export. Nationalization of the mines was one of the PU's first measures, and one of the biggest problems involved was the lack of Chilean technicians. The department of mining had existed for years, but was very weak, for political reasons — there were virtually no funds for it, as politicians had played along with the foreign-companies' opposition to the growth of national mining skills. The tacit view was that there were plenty of foreign technicians — hence our continuing dependence on companies which milked the country. So we planned a whole series of courses relating directly to copper mining, and thus to the Chilean economy.

There were many such changes in other fields, in medicine, education, art — all of them reversed since the coup. Two more of which I had some experience were journalism and social work. In journalism, much of the training was taken out of the University. Each group of students went with a teacher to a union branch or shantytown and started producing a paper with the local workers or residents, to deal with their particular problems. This taught the students that a journalist's job wasn't simply to hand news down to the people, but to get them to express themselves, through a medium which they controlled. These papers became a regular feature of dozens of local organizations, however modest. Gradually the students would reduce their contributions, until the paper was self-sufficient. This gave a tremendous boost to popular communication, creative, political and purely informative. The workers who wrote in these papers used the style of their everyday life — which also widened the students' experience and sense of language. The papers themselves became a source of important changes suggested at a popular level. For instance, in one such news-sheet a housewife in one of the shantytowns produced some completely new ideas for improving local food distribution. They were discussed in the shantytown and eventually implemented. No public official could have devised them, because they depended on a knowledge of day-to-day problems and living conditions in the locality.

I also mentioned social work. Its traditional assumptions began to be questioned. In a capitalist society social work is seen as assistance: care of orphans and widows, dealing with personal problems etc. — in short enabling the individual to re-adapt to the society. But now a new premise was suggested: that the social worker should make society aware of its inadequacies towards such people, and help them to pressure society for a solution to their problems. And to do this collectively in class terms, through which social problems are traced to class structures, and their solutions to changes in them. So too with social psychology; for instance 'family problems' were shown to be the problems of families affected by a class position and its social consequences. This may sound high-flown but it gave a new meaning to very real problems like wife-beating and alcoholism. Both these fell sharply during this period.

There was also new emphasis on applied work. Each mining-engineering student had a spell in a mine like Chuquicamata, doing research on some technical problem. This became a required part of the course. Agronomy students were sent to the country to work on agrarian reform. State agencies like INDAP funded many of these projects, and their results were often applied with voluntary student labour. I was involved in one such programme, building new types of chicken coops in several agrarian reform centres. In time these projects got more sophisticated. By 1973 student research and voluntary labour were vital to big irrigation schemes. For instance that summer four thousand students worked on one in the Ligua valley, in northern Chile, for several weeks.

For many students this was also their first direct contact with workers and *campesinos*. University entrance was now easier for students of working-class origin, and courses were put on for workers, training them for participation and management in the nationalized sector. But three years was too short a time to change the class nature of the university, although the students' federation did secure some modifications. Among them were courses in basic medicine, to train people from the shantytowns to man the local clinics; and in Concepción the university did admit a large number of workers, particularly for technical courses. Also traditional class relations within the university were challenged by the introduction of measures for the participation of non-academic staff — caretakers, office-workers and cleaners — in the running of the university. They got 10 per cent of the votes on committees, as against the students' 25 per cent and 65 per cent for the teaching staff. This also had a limited impact. The class nature of academic studies made it hard for them to have much to say. Yet it did produce direct contact and some political cooperation between student leaders and workers. And the latter were able to wield some influence even on matters like curriculum planning. The main changes were political, though, and also in simple class relationships. Many students were shaken, and their assumptions and life-styles changed, by meeting workers on a much more equal footing. For instance, traditional student parties became virtually limited to the right. People saw through their shallowness, because they now went to parties in the neighbourhoods where they were working politically. Quite apart from the principle, they found out how much more fun they were, which taught them something very new about the world they'd grown up in. Of course, none of these changes was isolated — by this time a number of former workers were deputies and ministers, so that traditional class relationships were being very widely shaken. Developments in the university did contribute to these changes, as well as being influenced by them.

*Political developments: polarization and debates on the
university left*

Following the presidential election, the left gained more
ground among the students, although it was always hard to
maintain, as student turnover was high and most still came
from conservative backgrounds. Experiences like voluntary
work often changed their consciousness radically. I remember one student who lived in the same shack as myself when
we were building the chicken coops. Seeing how left-wing
politics related to people's everyday problems overturned
her prejudices. She almost did believe that Communists ate
children on instructions from Moscow; she finally confided
in me about this and everything that she'd now learnt. Later
she became an activist of one of the PU parties. There were
hundreds of cases like this, of conversions based on simple
experience.

Yet this girl's background was typical, and to my mind
the left misled itself about the potential balance of forces
within the university. Most students' families became
increasingly conservative as Chilean society began to
polarize. I came from just such a family, well-off Christian
Democrats whose initial tolerance of my views grew weaker
as they saw that they were lasting. This meant that the
average new student from a petty-bourgeois background
became actively rather than passively conservative. However
naive this may have been, it meant that students were
increasingly hard to win over. And in time this was virtually
impossible, as the confrontation reached such a pitch that
few political meetings ended in anything but physical
conflict.

In 1970 or 1971 it was still possible for a good speaker to
hold an uncommitted audience, and even win some of it
over. But by 1973 such audiences hardly existed. Even when
students did have their eyes opened by voluntary work, for
instance, they now had to leap a much wider gap to join the
left, so few of them did so. By this time fascist groups and

doctrines were highly organized and explicit: almost anything the left said was systematically depicted as part of a plot directed by Moscow.

Clearly then, we'd lost the initiative. To my mind this dated from late 1971, when the extreme left started pressing for more radical transformations of the content of university teaching. These tactics split many faculties in half and virtually halted the university. This parallels the position of the ultra-left in other fields, but the university was their laboratory, which made it the same for right-wing parties, with their counter-revolution. In this confrontation the Christian Democrats and National Party allied with one another. Their strength was increasingly apparent. In early 1972 elections were held for a new rector. Although the PU candidate was moderate, the opposition candidate won, because the right and the centre had united. They were soon to do so nationally — and this election was very much a national issue, televised throughout the country as a political barometer. This was a serious loss for the left and one from which we never recovered, as it gave the initiative to the right. The National Party revived within the university, and by 1973 the fascist Fatherland and Freedom party was making progress with some students.

From this point on each faculty was controlled either by the right or the left. Life became one long confrontation. This and the increasing conservatism of new students made it a depressing field in which to be politically active. This reinforced the tendency of members of the other left parties to work outside the university, having failed to radicalize it. The Communist Party, though, still felt it was crucial and carried on in spite of these problems. In veterinary studies and law, for example, the fascists acquired such control that by 1973 left-wing students could hardly enter the buildings. If they did get into a class they were usually spotted and thrown out. Even where the balance was equal, left-wingers could study only at the price of daily confrontations. From almost the moment when the right took a stand, student politics meant violence. First the fascists persuaded the Christian Democrats to support their tactic of occupying various faculties. Initially the left held back, until finally the engineering faculty was occupied. This was so important to the economy that all the left decided it had to be retaken. The resulting battle lasted four hours, with hundreds involved on either side. The police kept out of it, as did the government, although PU parties had given the order to resist any further take-overs. Again the whole country was watching the outcome — even this was televised. It ended when the left had stormed the Fatherland and Freedom headquarters, but as they came up through an underground passage, the fascists threw nitric acid at them. Several people were badly burnt.

From this point on almost every meeting ended in fighting, sometimes with two thousand students involved. It's hard to say who came off better, but politically it was what the right was after, and so they gained ground. And of course there were differences within the left. To my mind we were especially weakened by this question of how much importance to attach to university politics. As I said, our student activists stuck to them, while those of other left parties, including the MIR, went to other fronts, among workers and *campesinos*. This was partly because of their shortage of activists among these sectors, but we Communists opposed this tactic in principle as well as practice. It weakened these parties' contribution to the university struggle, and we criticized this strongly.

We did manage to maintain a united facade. Before any mass student meeting the PU parties would always confer and agree to have a single speaker put forward a united position. But in fact we usually had differences, reflecting those at a national level — which made for heated discussions. Often our so-called united positions were just informative, or at best minimal agreements, rather than truly political positions. For instance the concept of popular power always generated controversy. It came to a head in the first bosses' strike of 1972, and was always contentious thereafter. Our position was that popular power already existed, so that we should be consolidating, not inventing new versions of it. It existed in that the PU existed as a workers' government; also in that the CUT existed as a central workers' organization; in the sense that there were countless, recognized working-class organizations, the JAPs for instance. To me it's a fallacy to say that the Communist Party obstructed popular power — the very election of Allende was a huge step in that direction. But there was often debate on this. I remember, for instance, how it once disrupted a meeting on how our faculty could support an industrial cordon called O'Higgins, which the Party was starting to organize. When we raised the issue of worker-student solidarity, the Socialist Party comrades demanded that the principle of popular power should be the focus of discussion — whereas we were concerned with the practical solidarity actions.

The point is that such solidarity did exist, however fragile. It existed in students' recognition that a revolutionary process was occurring, and that they should therefore defend the government. Several times in 1973, when the right was breaking up our meetings, we turned to nearby construction workers to support us — and they did. The fascists would turn tail and we were able to go on speaking. Worker-student solidarity was a popular phrase, but it meant something only when workers and students had common interests. As we saw it in the Party, the way to promote it was to unite behind the aims of the working class, which were enshrined in the PU's programme. This meant persuading students to campaign in the elections, to do voluntary work and help the PU to maintain production. The ultra-left's proposal for worker-student solidarity was to integrate the university with the cordons. But this was utopian — for one thing not all cordons were representative, to our way of thinking. Also there were differences between the PU parties as to what the cordons really were, how they should be constituted, what role they should play. The whole question was highly complex, so that the ultra-left's position of integrating with them was vague. We should join in organizing, but organizing exactly what? Organization, popular power, but what did this mean in real terms? It seemed to involve the notion that the cordons were nascent soviets, but this wasn't how we saw them. Though some students did participate in them, the federation never did in Santiago or Concepción, where this was also much discussed. What we did was to cooperate with them to defend the government as it required.

The end of the ball: students defend the PU

In the first bosses' strike, though, there was no doubt about the need to defend the government. Students threw themselves into the struggle, in the university and outside it. Students' PU committees tried to keep classes running normally and to provide workers' organizations with whatever help they requested. Each morning began with a mass meeting when the latest information was given, and then brigades were assigned to tasks of immediate urgency. Literally thousands of students signed on as emergency drivers for the convoys keeping supplies on the move, food, fuel and raw materials; others were assigned to defending warehouses, and loading and unloading supplies. Also we did our best to keep the university running. The right was trying to bring every faculty to a halt as well as cripple the economy. This mean weeks of physical confrontations as the right disrupted the classes of professors who were still teaching. Often we had to surround the buildings and remove the rightists first in order to get access to them. Hundreds of students were involved in these confrontations, with everything short of firearms — benches, chairs, tables, sticks. Any number of students were injured.

Outside the university the situation was equally violent, as we were trying to keep the economy going. Student brigades went out in answer to requests from the CUT or directly from factories needing help. I don't know how many sacks of flour and sugar I loaded and unloaded in those weeks, and like the workers we were constantly under attack. One convoy I went on, from Santiago to Melipilla, was blocked with trucks parked across the highway by landowners and lorry-drivers under the direction of the fascists. They outnumbered us. We were pulled out of the trucks, two students were killed and they took two Panamanians who were with us — being coloured, they took them for Cubans — and broke their arms. Any non-Chilean Latin American was a Cuban in their eyes, whether he came from Venezuela, Central America, they were all 'Cubans'.

We were also involved in requisitioning commercial establishments which closed down in support of the stoppage. The Department of Industry and Commerce could authorize this for any establishment which sold basic necessities. The Department would call the Federation: 'Comrades, we need a hundred and fifty students in Bolivar Street at ten o'clock, because we're going to requisition the store at number 57.' Whenever we could, we in the Federation provided the number of students requested. Departmental officials and police would arrive, with the power to nominate 'intervenors' to run the requisitioned concern. Often students were nominated. This also meant clashes with the right. When they were well armed, we had to pull back. This happened with one requisitioning, in which I took part, of a supermarket in an upper-class residential district. They asked us for only fifty students, and we arrived to find three hundred fascists waiting. Well, we knew the game was up, so we decided to get out while we could, but I was up front and they cut us off. One of them must have recognized me, I heard him shout: 'There's the boss, the Commie, get him.' I saw the sticks coming down on my head and that was about the last I knew of it. Luckily the police pulled me out of it. They bundled us all into a police van, and there we were, just two of us and six of them. By now it was night, and completely dark, and the fascists were banging at the door. 'They're in there, the Commie bastards, kill them.' When we got back a few hours later, our comrades had given us up for dead.

We lost this battle because it was in a fancy area. There were similar ones every day, but in other areas the outcome was different. I remember another in the city centre, by one of the new underground sites. This time the fascists hadn't done their reconnoitering. When we and the officials arrived, the fascists were waiting as usual, thinking that they had us outnumbered — then suddenly, just as they laid into us, dozens of construction workers appeared, with picks and shovels at the ready. In two minutes there wasn't a fascist to be seen. Clashes like this were daily events throughout the stoppage of October. Another job in which students helped was checking prices for the JAPs, to report black-market operators. I was once assigned to checking butchers, and had to retreat from their meat choppers until I learnt to make an inspection when plenty of customers were present, as they were usually sympathetic.

The stoppage was a turning point which made the forces involved more apparent. So many dollars were pouring in from CIA sources to back the striking lorry-owners that the dollar's black market price fell sharply. Many students' sympathy was turned into a firm commitment. Previous hesitators made up their minds and stood firm right into the coup and after, by that time at the risk of their lives. In the university all dialogue ended. Nothing could escape politics, which now simply meant confrontation. Shortly after the stoppage, the students' beauty contest was held. Among the finalists one was a known PU supporter, so PU activists campaigned for her. The results were due a few days later at a university ball, with thousands dancing and awaiting the result. The selection committee included several political leaders. They took seven hours to reach a decision! The left's candidate was the winner. Immediately it was announced, fights broke out among the dancers. That was the end of the ball.

The first stoppage proved the government's strength. Not only workers, but the army and the Church stood by it, and while the latters' support soon weakened, the workers stood firm. The right's attempt to turn the stoppage of El Teniente copper miners into a general strike was a failure. Not a single factory backed them. The clearest indication of growing popular awareness was in the congressional elections of March 1973. I campaigned with a party candidate in Santiago. The response was unprecedented. With the level of political discussions in the shantytowns and factories, we knew we were making massive gains, despite the inflationary effects of the bourgeoisie's economic boycott. Our vote went up by 20 per cent over the 1970 total — more evidence that despite the right's sabotage, we were winning at a democratic level. Although they still controlled the media, we exposed them constantly. Whenever we discovered a store which was hoarding and selling at black-market prices, it would be publicly denounced, including the commodities involved. People would then flock to buy them, and we'd improvise a political meeting, pointing out that the economic problems weren't caused by the government, as the right claimed, but by this deliberate hoarding. We'd repeat that the government was trying to control this, but that Congress was blocking its measures — so who was causing the so-called shortage? These exposure tactics were highly successful. Women, especially, changed their loyalties in favour of the PU once they realized what was happening. Again, the right's only answer was violence. They attacked queues of shoppers outside establishments known to be hoarding. They constantly assaulted JAP officials responsible for price-controlling. They gave out rival food supplies with propaganda tucked into the parcels. It was obvious what was happening, and they were losing votes by it daily.

To my mind the biggest demonstration ever of support for the PU, a measure of genuine workers' power, also came in these final months. After the El Teniente strike, the CUT called for a one-day stoppage to show the right that Chilean workers were with the PU and that there was no chance of winning them over. The stoppage was total. Student participation in that day's demonstration was massive. We assembled in every faculty to march to the centre of Santiago. The right had also organized a march, from El Teniente, which was supposed to end in the square in front of the Moneda Palace, to demand Allende's resignation. But they never got there. We dispersed them in the morning, and the left held the square — it was cold and raining, but the elation was tremendous, with Allende coming out to speak from the balcony every twenty or thirty minutes. Although the right tried to break us up, we controlled the situation completely. Workers from different industries manned each street to the Moneda by the hundreds, in perfect order. The construction workers even turned up with their cement-mixers and swore to use them to defend Allende and the constitution! The whole day through only one person died, in a shoot-out at the edge of the crowd. As I said, it was the clearest expression of popular power in all those three years.

The *tancazo* came a week later. The left was totally unprepared for it. As I arrived at the university I heard someone shouting: 'The tanks are round the Moneda, they're firing.' I'd never expected it. I ran to the Party youth headquarters, where they told us to wait in our places of study for further orders. So we went back. The faculty was already occupied, the fascists had been turned out. We waited there, organized into brigades and prepared to hold out, though we had no means of armed resistance. In the afternoon we were told that things were under control and that there would be a demonstration in front of the Moneda that evening. By seven we were there, and again there was an enormous crowd, and Allende spoke, though to my mind wrongly, repeating that all was under control. We all went home under that impression.

It soon became clear that this wasn't the case. That same

night there were more rumours of a coup — and there were meetings in the barracks, but nothing immediate came of them. I believe that at this point the PU leadership, above all Allende himself, failed to act firmly. The plotters should have been purged from the armed forces, not placated, though I wouldn't agree with those who demanded the closure of Congress. From having never expected a coup we now went to the opposite extreme — four out of every five nights or so there were alerts. From the end of June right up to the coup we were called out almost every night to defend our places of work and study. So that when the crunch came on the night of the tenth, no one believed it! Or rather, we believed it was coming, but by that time we were so exhausted that the warnings were ineffective.

The approach of the coup: the student response to the narrowing of the PU's options

After the *tancazo* the PU decided to organize defence brigades throughout the country. There was also a proposal for another march in Santiago, to let the right know that if they were planning civil war, the PU was ready. It was all arranged and I was involved as a representative of the Students' Federation. But the march was called off — it was national flag day, and the armed forces were due to parade in Santiago. This was another show of weakness.

The defence brigades went ahead, though. The MIR wanted to call them 'committees for the defence of the revolution', as in Cuba. The students took part, but this scheme was limited; it was seen only as a means of supporting a hoped-for division within the armed forces. Also it was far from efficient — as we discovered after the coup, when various infiltrators denounced us. But the crucial point was that we'd lost the battle for the loyalty of the armed forces. It was this which turned the balance of power against us, in the university as outside it. The right was gaining ground everywhere, except of course among the workers, but this left them isolated, as the second stoppage in July and August showed. We couldn't fight back and keep things going as we had before. We tried to carry out the same tasks, but the middle class had now been won over by the centre-right alliance of Christian Democrats and Nationalists. Again we sent out working brigades, but tasks like unloading and loading the trucks were now impossible. The army and police no longer protected us. At times they even prevented us from working. What could we do? The convoys became impossible — we were shot at on every corner, and shooting back would have been suicidal. Transport ground to a halt, the shops closed and the university was paralysed. With the left's indecision at a national level, the middle ground could see no way out — it was either civil war or the coup. The only alternative was some new step, like a plebiscite. But I doubt if even this was possible. Had the left won it, the military would still have intervened, arguing fraud by the PU. Pinochet said as much after the coup. There was no way out, no solution that the PU could offer. Its fall was only a matter of time.

The threats and repression of students began before the coup. Since the *tancazo* I'd had threatening calls and letters — the scraps of paper with 'Jakarta' written on them, to remind us of the massacre of Communists in Indonesia. Two of our comrades were said to have been caught with plans of some barracks. They were tortured and gave details of our organization. On the tenth there was a final clash between right and left in the university. That night we held another meeting to discuss the military's position, but we could see no way out. Next morning we controlled most faculties, and were still prepared to defend the government, through the brigades set up for this purpose. I was at party headquarters as the first news of the coup came through. They gave us the same instructions — to await orders for our part in the plans for defending the whole of Chile. Naturally there were such plans, but they were based on the assumption that some of the military would remain loyal. By eleven the faculty was beginning to be surrounded. The parties debated whether to stay or retire to key sectors. There were about five hundred of us, students and university workers, all ready to resist if we could have. But finally the PU ordered us to retire in our brigades to private houses in the city. There was resistance on some campuses, but it was isolated and crushed.

We stayed in hiding in brigades for some days, still organized and awaiting instructions. Our structure at the base was virtually intact, but we had nothing clear to act on. We were still in touch with one another, but cut off from the leadership. We realized that there was widespread resistance — we could hear fighting in the streets — but all of it seemed to reflect the same thing, a lack of any coordination. We showed our faces only once, when we went to one of the shantytowns to get a comrade's family out, because we'd heard it was going to be bombed. The Air Force had sent a search party there on the previous night, and they'd all been killed and their uniforms taken — the bodies were still there. This type of resistance was going on everywhere, but all of it seems to have been spontaneous. Contrary to what people think, there was some local coordination between all the left-wing parties, but it was only fragmentary, as all of them were cut off from their leaders.

Later, when I did get personal instructions, I was told to keep low because I was marked. I did so for a month, moving from one place to another, then I tried visiting the university. But I was immediately denounced and arrested. Like almost everyone else, I was tortured. More than some, less than many. How I got out I obviously can't tell, but I was told that I had no option but to leave Chile.

What we had suffered was a defeat — not to my mind because of our differences, but because of the forces we faced. There was no immediate answer to them, though certainly mistakes were made. Particularly over the armed forces, and in our failure to control the media, which weighed heavily against us. Yet I still believe that it was an advance, through the new awareness which Chileans gained, and imperialism's loss of prestige, in counting on fascist counter-measures. It was the same with the Vietnamese war, and look at the outcome. With each act of oppression, imperialism loses ground in the long term, especially in Latin America. That's why I believe that the next round is ours.

Personally, I changed in those years. I realize now that I joined the Party thinking I had something to teach it. But I discovered that history isn't as I'd imagined it, the product of political leadership by the conventionally wise. I found instead that it's made by an anonymous people at a level far deeper than that of political petty-bourgeois, supposed intelligence. I found that this people has a knowledge and strength — to organize and make decisions — which I'd never dreamed of, which came to light under the PU. I discovered the awareness of people who would queue for hours without protest, in the conviction that come what may they had to keep struggling for the PU. Not out of obstinacy or blindness, as intellectuals might suppose, but out of the awareness they'd won. Not just in those years, but through generations. I came to understand Chilean history in ways I'd read of, but never quite grasped, as the history of a people's genuine struggles. I realised what the Party meant to such people, from being rooted in their past, even to non-members of it. And this was because it had grown over years through conversations and conversions, with each struggle adding to the whole, despite a totally hostile setting. I realized that it was this people's movement which lay behind the PU — a people who knew that waiting in a queue for hours was no hardship compared to the years of struggle behind it. This is why I'm convinced, quite objectively, that this awareness, and the left parties, will survive, not just in a few people's minds but as the product of this history. However many people the fascists have slaughtered and however many more they slaughter, they'll never destroy it, this force that we felt in every queue, in

every meeting, even when times were hardest. This is why
the repression is so severe; but it also means that the left will
never abandon the struggle. And this isn't something I
learnt as a student, but as an activist, from the people.

Abbreviations and Glossary

Administrative Council. See *General Administrative Council.*

Asentamiento Literally 'settlement', untranslated in text because of specific connotations as unit of agrarian reform introduced by Christian Democrats. Designed on basically cooperative lines, but including option of sub-division of land among individual members and employment by them of wage labour.

Campamento Literally 'encampment', untranslated in text because of specific connotations as *shantytown* involving a degree of organization generally deriving from the land occupation with which it originated.

Campesino Country person, rather than 'peasant' in the narrower sense, i.e. all categories of agricultural workers, from wage-earners to small tenants and share-croppers. Untranslated in text for want of exact equivalent in English.

Campesino council (*Consejo Campesino*) Local joint organization of all categories of *campesinos* distinct from *campesino* unions (*sindicatos*). (The latter involved mainly rural wage workers and affiliation to the CUT, whereas the councils were autonomous.) In practice heavily supported by the left of the PU, as the vehicle of agrarian policies distinct from those of the Communist-led CUT.

CDP Committee for the Defence of Production (*Comité de Defensa de la Producción*). Rank and file workers' committee of type established in factories by the more left-wing PU parties, initially to counter sabotage and cutbacks of production, and more independent of union control than the official *Production Committees*.

CERA Agrarian Reform Centre (*Centro de Reforma Agraria*). Unit of agrarian reform introduced by PU along more collective lines than the Christian Democrats' *asentamientos*.

Communal Command (*Comando Comunal*) Local joint associations of factory workers, shantytown dwellers and *campesinos*, generally originating from *industrial cordons*.

CORA Agrarian Reform Corporation (*Corporación de Reforma Agraria*) Government department responsible for legal and technical aspects of land reform.

Cordon See *Industrial Cordon*.

CORFO Industrial Development Corporation (*Corporación de Fomento*). Government body originally established by the Popular Front Government of the 1930s to encourage local industry with technical advice and credit.

CUT Central Workers' Confederation (*Central Única de Trabajadores*). Equivalent in Chile to British TUC.

ENAMI National Mining Enterprise (*Empresa Nacional de Minería*). Government department responsible for technical aid to mining sector.

General Administrative Council (*Consejo General de Administración*). Management committee of industries in public sector, as officially constituted by PU.

Hectare (*Hectarea*) Basic unit of land measurement, equivalent to 2.4 acres.

INDAP Agrarian Development Institute (*Instituto de*

Desarollo Agro-Pecuario). Government department responsible mainly for social aspects of agrarian development.

Intervenor (*Interventor*) Interim government manager of firms taken over by government in the event of long-term technical, financial or labour relations problems.

Industrial Cordon (*Cordón Industrial*) Local association of workers in neighbouring factories, developed mainly in response to the right-wing stoppages of 1972-3. In this context officially recognized by the PU, but mainly promoted by elements of the Socialist Party, MAPU, Christian Left and MIR as the keystone of popular power and embryo of communal commands. As such, regarded with some unease by the Communist Party as a challenge to the official trades-union structure.

JAP People's Supply Control Committee (*Junta de Abastecimiento Popular*) Local consumer organization established under the PU mainly to counter black-market operations.

*MAPU Movement of Popular United Action (*Movimiento de Acción Popular Unitario*).

*MIR Revolutionary Left Movement (*Movimiento de Izquierda Revolucionario*).

*MOC Worker-*Campesino* Movement (*Movimiento Obrero-Campesino*).

National Agricultural Society (*Sociedad Nacional de Agricultura*) Large landowners' association, which acted increasingly as the focus of right-wing mobilization against the PU in the countryside.

Neighbourhood Association (*Junta de Vecinos*) Residents' pressure groups, particularly in shantytowns, set up either spontaneously or by political parties to campaign for local facilities and legal land titles etc.

*For information on these and other political parties, see Introduction.

Popular power (*Poder Popular*) A major slogan and strategy of the left of the PU and the MIR, for the devolution of power to grassroots organizations such as the industrial cordons and communal commands. As such, the main concept round which debate within the PU centred.

Production Committee (*Comité de Producción*) Factory committee set up under the PU's scheme for workers' participation, to monitor production levels (cf. CDP.)

Ranquil Campesino confederation originally founded in 1930s and controlled by the Communist and Socialist parties. Named after the site of a famous confrontation between *campesinos*, landowners and the police in southern Chile (cf. *Triunfo Campesino* and Worker-*Campesino* Unity below).

Shantytown (*Población*) Low-income urban housing area, resulting generally from land occupations, often organized by political parties (cf. *Campamento*).

Tancazo Literally 'tank attack', untranslated in text, where it refers to the attempted coup of 29 June 1973, so called because it was led by a tank regiment which surrounded the Presidential Palace.

Triunfo Campesino Literally '*Campesino* Triumph', left untranslated in text. The main Christian Democrat controlled *campesino* confederation, founded in the 1960s on the strength of the Christian Democrats' land reforms. As such it tended to represent the conservative, medium to small-scale peasantry won over by the attractions of land reform on an individualist, capitalist, rather than collective basis (cf. *Ranquil* and *Worker*-Campesino *Unity*).

Worker-Campesino *Unity* (*Confederación Unidad Obrero-Campesino*) *Campesino* confederation instigated by the MAPU in 1971 as a breakaway from *Triunfo Campesino* to support agrarian policies more radical than those of *Ranquil*.

Chronology of Political Events
in the PU Period

1970

January

PU coalition announces candidacy of Allende for presidential elections

Jorge Alessandri and Radomiro Tomic nominated as candidates for National Party and Christian Democrats respectively

September

Presidential elections; PU wins 36 per cent of vote, National Party 34 per cent, Christian Democrats 28 per cent; US columnist Jack Anderson later reveals unsuccessful ITT (International Telephone and Telegraphy Corporation) collusion with Christian Democrats and Chilean financial interests to prevent congressional ratification

US State Department expresses 'dismay' at Allende's victory

Run on banks starts financial panic

Christian Democrats demand Allende's agreement to 'statute of guarantees' for existing freedoms and legalities, including 'integrity of armed forces'

October

Allende signs statutes of guarantees; Congress ratifies his election

Suspension of US aid to Chile

Fascist Fatherland and Freedom Party attempts unsuccessfully to kidnap army C-in-C General Schneider, in hope of provoking coup; Schneider killed (CIA involvement later revealed in US Senate hearings)

November

Allende inaugurated

Release of all political prisoners; MIR announces 'critical support' for PU

Diplomatic relations restored with Cuba

December

Land occupations by *campesinos* in south

1971

January

Copper nationalization bill; announcement of plans to nationalize coal mines and all banks

February

Announcement of plans to nationalize nitrate industry

First symptoms of internal economic boycotts as cattle-ranchers drive their herds into Argentina

March

Hostile comments on Chile in Nixon's foreign-policy statement

Government begins take-over of mainly US-owned copper mines

April

Municipal elections; PU wins 50.9 per cent of votes; Christian Democrats and National Party present some joint candidates for first time, winning 44.6 per cent

May

First nationalizations of major industries (mainly textile) other than copper

June

Leaders of *campesino* land occupations clash with police

July

Copper nationalization bill unanimously ratified by Congress

August

Formation of Christian Left Party within PU, combining breakaway Christian Democrats and former members of MAPU not committed to Marxist-Leninist position

Minority section of Radical Party leaves PU to form Radical Left Party, aligned with Christian Democrats

October

US copper companies denounce PU compensation terms, which include deductions for excess profits and illegal operations

Government defines proposed public, mixed and private sectors of economy, with former specifying size of companies for nationalization — these would amount to 150 in all

November

Fidel Castro visits Chile

December

Right-wing mass mobilization begins, with 'march of the empty cooking pots' by wealthy Santiago housewives in protest against shortages caused by increased demand, due to rising wages

1972

January

First of many Christian Democrat-led congressional censures of PU ministers forces resignation of Jorge Toha, Minister of Interior; on his reappointment to Cabinet, Christian Democrats announce future non-cooperation with government

February

Government specifies 120 companies due for nationalization; Congress passes measures severely restricting legal basis for further nationalizations

US court freezes New York funds of Chilean public agencies in retaliation for PU indemnification terms for US companies

March

CUT promises workers' active support of government's nationalization programme

Details published of ITT involvement in attempts to prevent Allende's ratification; ITT admits authenticity

April

Moderate PU candidate defeated in symptomatic election for rector of University of Chile

May

Confrontation in Concepción between MIR and right-wing activists

June

Talks between government and Christian Democrats, opposed by sectors of PU

Dismissal of Pedro Vuskovic, Economics Minister, closely associated with nationalizations and heavily attacked in right-wing propaganda

July

Suspension of talks between government and Christian Democrats; Christian Democrats and National Party announce joint platform for next year's congressional elections

In Concepción MIR and sectors of PU hold a Popular Assembly, criticized by Communist Party as departure from legality

August

Renewed right-wing demonstrations against government include participation by some Christian Democrat workers

September

Kennecott Corporation brings successful legal action in France for seizure of Chilean copper cargo, pending settlement of dispute over indemnification

Attacks on left-wing radio stations; street clashes between right and left in Santiago and Concepción during anniversary celebrations of 1970 elections

October

Beginning of strike by Christian Democrat-controlled lorry-owners' confederation, allegedly over lack of spare parts; shopkeepers and some professionals join strike; state of emergency declared to deal with economic crisis; Christian Democrats refuse discussion of crisis with government; factories threatened with closure occupied and maintained by workers

Army C-in-C General Prats reaffirms constitutional role of military

November

Kennecott persuades Dutch and Canadian banks to suspend loans to Chile

New Cabinet appointments include three military officers,

among them Prats as Minister of Interior; Christian Left
  Cabinet members resign over government's 'conciliation'
End of lorry-owners' strike

December
US breaks off talks with Chile to renegotiate debt repayments

1973

January
PU proposes state control of distribution of agricultural
  products; protests from business organizations

February
Congressional election campaign; PU programme based on
  proposals to further socialize economy and substitute a
  Popular Assembly for current legislature, with legislation
  to be initiated by CUT and/or popular demand

March
Congressional elections; PU increases its vote by 20 per cent
  over 1970 (some 7 per cent of total vote) but with 43.4 per
  cent is still short of majority required for implementation
  of proposals, while right is far short of two-thirds required
  for proposed impeachment of Allende
Section of MAPU breaks away to form MOC, in close align-
  ment with Communist Party
Replacement by civilians of military ministers

April
Strike at El Teniente copper mine, where workers demand
  wage increases
Talks with US on renegotiation of debt again break down
  over US demands for prior compensation of copper
  companies
Congress opposes Bill for further nationalizations

May
Armed confrontations between MIR and Fatherland and
  Freedom Party; large arms caches discovered in latter's
  headquarters

June
Congress opposes Bill for lowering limit of farm expropriations from eighty to forty hectares and forces further
  ministerial resignations
Assassination attempt on Prats, now clearly identified as
  leader of non-interventionists in armed forces
Tancazo (tank regiment revolt), supported by Fatherland
  and Freedom Party; workers resist with factory occupations; revolt put down within a few hours; Congress
  refuses Allende's request for full emergency powers
End of El Teniente strike
Renewal of lorry-owners' strike, allegedly in protest at lack
  of spares but also against PU proposals for state transport
  system

July
Sectors of CUT dispute government decision to return to
  owners factories occupied during *tancazo*
Allende agrees to Christian Democrat demand for implementation by army of laws for arms searches; Allende
  and Christian Democrats reopen talks for constitutional
  solution of political crisis

August
Christian Democrats break off talks with Allende and declare
  support for lorry-owners' strike
Shopkeepers and professional groups join lorry-owners'
  strike in increasing numbers; strike leaders demand
  government's resignation
Sabotage on power lines and railways
Arms search laws increasingly used by military to intimidate
  workers

Three military men, including Prats, join Cabinet

Sailors and workers at Valparaiso naval base denounce plans for coup by navy; Cabinet criticized for lack of action over their detention and torture by naval intelligence

Armed confrontation between Communist Party and Christian Democrat supporters in neighbourhood of Congress, which accuses Allende of violating constitution; deputies call on armed forces 'to choose between executive and legislature'

Resignation of military Cabinet members; Prats also resigns as C-in-C of army; Allende charges opposition with risking civil war and encouraging military intervention

Right-wing papers and radio station openly demand military intervention; Congress rejects Bill for their closure

Mounting sabotage and terrorism, especially by Fatherland and Freedom Party

September

Demonstration in Santiago in support of PU on third anniversary of elections reckoned at half a million people; Allende warns of plot to overthrow PU

Allende appeals to Christian Democrats for resumption of talks; they reply with demands for his resignation

On the eleventh PU overthrown by coordinated military coup; Allende and advisers killed, following Air Force attack on Moneda Palace; sporadic armed resistance, mass arrests and executions, banning of all left-wing political parties, suspension of basic democratic and human rights; declaration by General Pinochet, leader of new military junta, of intention to 'eliminate every trace of Marxism from Chile'

Postscript

Events in Chile since the overthrow of the Popular Unity

Since the coup censorship in Chile has stifled most sources of information. Among the surviving publications, only the Jesuit *Mensaje* is independent and reliable. Moreover, this gap has been filled by a Kafka-esque web of misinformation. Even reports which might at first seem favourable to the left or prejudicial to the junta are sometimes concocted by the DINA (*Departamiento de Inteligencia Nacional*), the National Intelligence Agency. In addition to tales of armed resistance, to justify new waves of detentions, it has also spread stories of repression bizarre enough to undermine all credibility on the subject. The information which follows is therefore based on established international sources, such as *Le Monde*, the London weekly *Latin America*, and United Nations publications. *Chile Monitor* and the declarations of the Chilean left have only been used, and that discreetly, for information on the left itself. This is understandably muted.

The Consolidation of the Junta

The junta established by the coup consists of the heads of the armed forces — the army, navy, air force and police (*carabineros*). Its evident leader from the outset, army

General Pinochet, was soon appointed president. He rules by decree, with the help since 1975 of a 'consultative council'. Largely nominated by Pinochet, this can only consider the junta's proposals and has no more than advisory powers. The junta's first measures effectively outlawed the left and the labour movement. The CUT, most trades union confederations and all left-wing political parties were banned. The other parties were suspended. The electoral rolls were officially burned. Pinochet has consistently repeated that the junta will retain power indefinitely.

Its policies have gone far beyond the reversal of the Popular Unity's advances. The coup's violence, despite the lack of resistance, was clearly a political project. It was designed to create the conditions to physically eliminate the left and reintroduce free enterprise to a degree unknown in Chile since the 1930s. Whilst the CIA was instrumental in this process, according to a US Senate enquiry, its explicit mentor is the University of Chicago monetarist and Nobel prize-winner, Milton Friedman. His 'social market economy' has meant extensive denationalization and savage cuts in public spending. Many state agencies long pre-dating the Popular Unity, CORA, INDAP and CORFO among them, have been virtually dismantled. Employment in the public sector has been cut by a third. Private foreign investment has been invited on terms so favourable that Chile has left the Andean Pact with neighbouring countries, which limits profit remissions and so on.

The returns as yet are virtually nil. Many small firms have gone to the wall, and even copper has suffered a recession. With the banning of strikes, collective bargaining and the election of trades union officials, the real basic wage has fallen by fifty per cent, according to *Mensaje* and other sources. The latest official figure for unemployment (the lowest of many) is nineteen per cent, compared to just over three per cent during most of the Popular Unity period. The junta apparently aspires to emulate the growth produced by the similar Brazilian 'model'. Yet growth in Brazil (which has since declined) was based on very different conditions — the repression of the living standards of a much less organized working class, more sophisticated management, a boom in the international economy and a much larger local market. Far from growing, output in Chile has fallen steadily since the coup — by some fifteen per cent in 1975 alone, according to World Bank calculations. The only marked increase is of food exports, which simply reflects a reduction of consumption in Chile. Actual agricultural production has fallen. Output of wheat, a staple foodstuff, has been halved since the Popular Unity period, according to official figures for the 1975/6 harvest. To put it bluntly, the outside world is eating Chileans' meals for them.

This means malnutrition of varying degrees for roughly half the population. Politically it has also meant the disenchantment with the junta of forces that were previously behind it, and typically of Christian Democrats. After the coup the official leadership of this largest single party declared in favour of the junta, but others dissociated themselves immediately or within a short while. These divisions have inevitably widened. For two years ex-president Eduardo Frei, the State Department and figures close to the junta itself, were apparently looking to Christian Democrats for some semi-civilian regime, again on the Brazilian model. However, in the circumstances of unrelieved economic collapse and growing repression, this proved impossible. As the junta's exclusively militarist wing under Pinochet gained the upper hand, reinforced by shifts to the right in other Latin American countries, potential leaders of any rapprochement were marginalized or eliminated. As early as 1974 the constitutionalist General Prats was assassinated in Buenos Aires. The civilian-oriented General Bonilla, Pinochet's second-in-command, died in mysterious circumstances. Innumerable generals have been retired. Dissident Christian Democrats have been gaoled in increasing numbers, and recently even Frei has complained of attempts on his life.

The implications of this polarization are much debated on the left, especially now that Frei has come out openly against the junta, with Pinochet surviving what was temporarily a crisis for him. The US response, on the other hand, since roughly mid 1975, has been to opt clearly to back Pinochet, whilst discreetly pressing for a better image on human rights questions. However, the end of the Kissinger era may call this policy into question.

Human rights and the repression

These developments have reinforced the junta's reliance on repression. The DINA, which coordinates it, is largely trained by Brazilian agents and responsible only to Pinochet, though as in Brazil it has its own links with right-wing terrorist organizations. Its brutality is now widely known. The personal experiences of many activists interviewed by us included every imaginable form of torture, mutilation and killing. As the subject has been documented elsewhere (for instance in Amnesty's *Chile. An Amnesty International Report*, London, 1974) we chose to omit it. The most reliable estimates of the number of people killed since the coup are in the region of 30,000 — which the junta itself has once admitted — though official figures usually put it lower. (The official 'state of internal war', permitting summary executions after brief hearings by war tribunals, lasted a year). Similar estimates of all those detained since September 1973 put the number at 150,000 — about one in forty of the adult population (though these figures also include the frequent re-arrest of the same persons). By mid 1976 some four thousand people were still officially detained. Releases since then have been offset by a rapid rise in the number of people just 'disappearing'. The number of such cases documented by Catholic sources is about two thousand. Refugees from Chile number over 100,000. The largest group, in Argentina, is subject to constant harassment, kidnappings and assassinations by right-wing terrorist groups in cooperation with the DINA. The latter also operates in Europe and the USA, and was almost certainly responsible for the car-bomb murder in Washington in September 1976 of ex-Popular Unity Minister Orlando Letelier.

Within Chile the liberal wing of the Church is virtually the only body which can blunt the edge of the repression. For two years an inter-denominational Peace Committee, led by the Cardinal, organized legal defence for prisoners and support for their families and those without work. However, as the Church became unavoidably outspoken at what it was witnessing, this was dissolved. Its work has continued on a denominational basis, but those involved, including priests, have themselves become victims of the repression.

In these circumstances the strongest protests have come from international sources. In the non-Communist world, almost every international body of standing, including the United Nations, The International Labour Organization, The International Commission of Jurists and Amnesty International, has condemned the torture and killing in Chile. Even the Organization of American States, at its 1976 annual meeting in Santiago, raised the issue. After Pinochet opened the proceedings with a renewed declaration of 'ideological warfare ... in defence of Western Christian civilization', the OAS Human Rights Commission condemned the junta's 'arbitrary gaolings, persecution and torture'. More importantly, the international labour movement has also been galvanized into action. As a result of its pressure, the governments of several Western countries, including Britain, Italy and Sweden, have either cut or severely curtailed their diplomatic relations with Chile. Even the Ford administration was forced by Congress to cut direct military aid to the junta, though this means in effect that it simply passes through third countries. By 1975 a number of European governments, including Britain's refused to renegotiate the junta's scheduled debt repayments.

For much of the labour movement, however, this was more than a question of human rights. It was also one of civil rights and the political future of Chile.

Debates on the left and the resistance to the junta

Both spontaneously and in response to a call from the Chilean CUT in exile, trade unionists throughout the world launched boycotts against trade with Chile. (Those in Britain are documented in the Chile Solidarity Campaign's *Chile Fights* special issue, 'Chile and the British Labour Movement' published in 1975.) Popular Unity leaders in exile set up a coordinating committee for their activities in Europe, which also cooperates with the MIR and dissident Christian Democrat exiles.

Whilst muted by the struggle for survival and reorganization, debates continue within the left about how best to resist the junta, and what strategies to follow. All left parties agreed immediately that spontaneous armed resistance was futile. The first steps toward an effective resistance were reorganization, propaganda, and the building of a popular movement against the policies of the Generals. This strategy would be reinforced by mobilizing world opinion to isolate them internationally. Initially the MIR, with some support from the parties close to it, laid more emphasis on early prospects of a popular insurrection. However, by 1975 many of its leaders had been killed or forced into exile, along with those of other left parties. The result is a measured rapprochement between them, after a fairly bitter period of retrospective recriminations on 'ultra-leftism' and 'reformism', encouraged by most of the left in Europe. This has now given way to a recognition, on the one hand, that tactical compromises are called for; and on the other, that the junta's weakness is no guarantee of political openings.

These questions crystallize round the issue of how to relate to the Christian Democrats. On the one hand there are evident grounds for building the broadest possible alliance, on a democratic platform, with all sectors opposed to the junta. These now include the bulk of the Christian Democrat Party. On the other hand 'democracy' is hardly a reliable platform, in the light of the Popular Unity experience, and Frei showed scant concern for it until he fell out with the junta. Chile's left has strong historical grounds for distrusting any such alliance, which led in the 1930s-40s to its marginalization and repression by the bourgeois parties which it had supported. More recently, though, it is also true that the splits in the Christian Democrats which produced the Christian Left and MAPU strongly reinforced the left, without involving compromises. The question, therefore, is whether to consider such an alliance with the party as a whole, with its dissident fractions, or with none of it — and on what terms?

The option commanding the widest support is now the second, of some relationship with dissident Christian Democrats, on terms whose general basis lies in the difference between the experiences of the 1930s and 1960s: and this is that the latter involved a winning over of much of the Christian Democrats' base to clearly socialist objectives. For this to be possible now, however, requires some tangible advance in the position of every party. The usually clichéd 'lessons of Chile' will have to be seen as lessons for all, not just for 'reformists' or 'ultra-leftists'. Whilst the 'new left' in Latin America since the Cuban revolution has failed to build a mass following for its analysis, much of it valid, the weakness of the Communist parties has been the reverse: the lack of a new analysis to make its undoubted base effective. No less important than the danger of a full-blooded bourgeois alliance is the fact that any 'vanguardism' without a massive popular base, and the tactical compromises entailed, affords no real prospects of power in the Latin American circumstances. Hints of this have come from both of what clearly remain the 'two sides' of the left. The Communist and Socialist parties have recognized their lack of an answer to 'the problem of the military' in the Popular

Unity period. The other parties do now seem prepared to conceive of relationships, if not alliances, with new forces. However, this is one thing at the level of general declarations. It still remains to translate these advances into practice, in the form of a concrete programme for Chile which goes some way beyond 'anti-fascist' positions.

Insofar as these problems are reflections of those of the international left, it may be naive to speculate on purely Chilean advances. However, it is also true that revolutions have been made by revolutionary practice, rather than debates in exile, whose significance is exaggerated by their being more conspicuous than concrete developments in Chile. That these involve few dramatic events is partly a measure of the left's success in working for reorganization and effective propaganda, rather than rapid confrontation. Two things stand out in the consequently scant information on the opposition to the junta — a new degree of cooperation between grassroots activists of different parties like those whose stories feature here; and widespread popular resistance to current policies, despite the penalties. For instance, all the left-wing parties are regularly producing and distributing clandestine news-sheets, presumably with a new generation reliving Gregorio's childhood experiences (chapter I) of this sort of political work. Even in gaol new bonds have been forged on the common anvil of the repression between activists with different experiences and political positions. Resistance committees also exist in many places of work and residence — and whilst the Chilean left in exile may disagree as to their merits, many of them are in fact inter-party. Rate strikes are occurring in shantytowns, stoppages in the copper mines, go-slows in the factories and ports. Wall slogans are reappearing — sometimes just 'R' for *'Resistencia'*.

All these of necessity involve substantial organization and awareness. They also suggest the experience and will of a new political generation committed, in some of Allende's last words, to new and appropriate forms of struggle.

What to read on Chile

A surprisingly difficult question. The coup has produced a spate of books and pamphlets, but little in English with any depth or originality. Most of them, like Helios Prieto's *Chile: The Gorillas Are Amongst Us*, (Pluto Press, 1974) are superficial and sectarian, of the 'told you so' variety. The one comprehensive study in depth of the Popular Unity and its background is *Chile: the State and the Revolution* by Ian Roxborough, Philip O'Brien and Jackie Roddick (Macmillan, 1976, paperback edition). This also has a comprehensive bibliography of books and articles in French and Spanish, as well as English. Otherwise, the most readable items published since the coup are probably *Revolution and Counter-revolution in Chile*, edited by Paul Sweezy and Harry Magdoff (Monthly Review Press, 1974) and Michel Raptis' book of the same name, sub-titled *A Dossier on Workers' Participation in the Revolutionary Process* (Allison and Busby, 1974). The first is a collection of articles written before and after the coup. The second includes valuable documentary material on the various popular organizations such as the industrial cordons, but not enough, whilst the author's comments, like most on the subject, are largely an affirmation of faith.

In these circumstances, the most vivid reading dates mainly from before the coup, though much of this is also one-sided. A prime example is Kate Clark's *Reality and Prospects of Popular Unity* (Lawrence and Wishart, 1973), which virtually ignores the controversy over the PU's strategy. Read together with Prieto it is a fair measure of how far Chile was a problem not just of imperialism, but of the sclerosis of the whole left, and not just in Chile. On the positive side, *The Chilean Road to Socialism*, edited by Ann Zammit (Institute of Development Studies, Sussex, 1973) includes discussions which remain live, however dated, and also the Popular Unity programme. Regis Debray's *Conversations with Allende* (New Left Books, 1971) is lively, despite Debray's arrogant moments. Allende's speeches are also vivid, seen in their context and with hindsight — *Chile's Road to Socialism*, Salvador Allende, ed. Juan Garces (Penguin, 1973). Sadly, though, the best books — those which argue issues openly, or provide the raw material for this — remain untranslated. Notable amongst them are 'The State and Tactical Problems During the Government of Allende' (*El Estado y Los Problemas Tacticos en el Gobierno de Allende*, Siglo Veintiuno, Madrid, 1974), also by Juan Garces, an advisor and close friend of Allende. And Maurice Najman's 'Chile is Close' (*Le Chili Est Proche*, Maspero, Paris, 1974), a much fuller collection of documents than Michel Raptis'. In confirmation of Najman's title, as measured a blow from the right as any is Robert Moss's *Chile's Marxist Experiment* (David and Charles, 1973). Full of misrepresentations and venom, it's a healthy reminder that Pinochet has friends in Britain.

On events since the coup the best informed source — though hitherto short on political analysis — is *Chile Monitor*, published roughly every two months by the Chile Solidarity Campaign in London. The NACLA (North American Congress on Latin America, N.Y. and Berkeley, California) *Latin America and Empire Report* for October 1973 ('Chile: the Story Behind the Coup') is still worth reading, whilst its November 1976 number (volume X, no. 9, 'Chile: recycling the capitalist crisis') gives the most thorough

up-to-date information at the time of writing. Most of
the Chilean left parties in exile are now publishing documents in English. However, they are understandably
guarded, and there is as yet no adequate analysis of them,
nor of the resistance in Chile. The commentators — and
perhaps the surviving leaders too — have yet to do justice
to the fallen.

Colin Henfrey
January 1977